DATE DUE

Brodart Co.   Cat. # 55 137 001   Printed in USA

RED ON WHITE

The Biography of Duke Redbird

by

Marty Dunn

1971

new press

toronto

Copyright 1971. The poems in this book are copyright 1971 by Duke Redbird. The text of the book is copyright by Marty Dunn. No part of this book may be reproduced in any form without permission in writing from the original publishers, new press, Toronto, Canada.
ISBN 0 88770-009-8
new press 84 Sussex Avenue Toronto
Printed in Canada

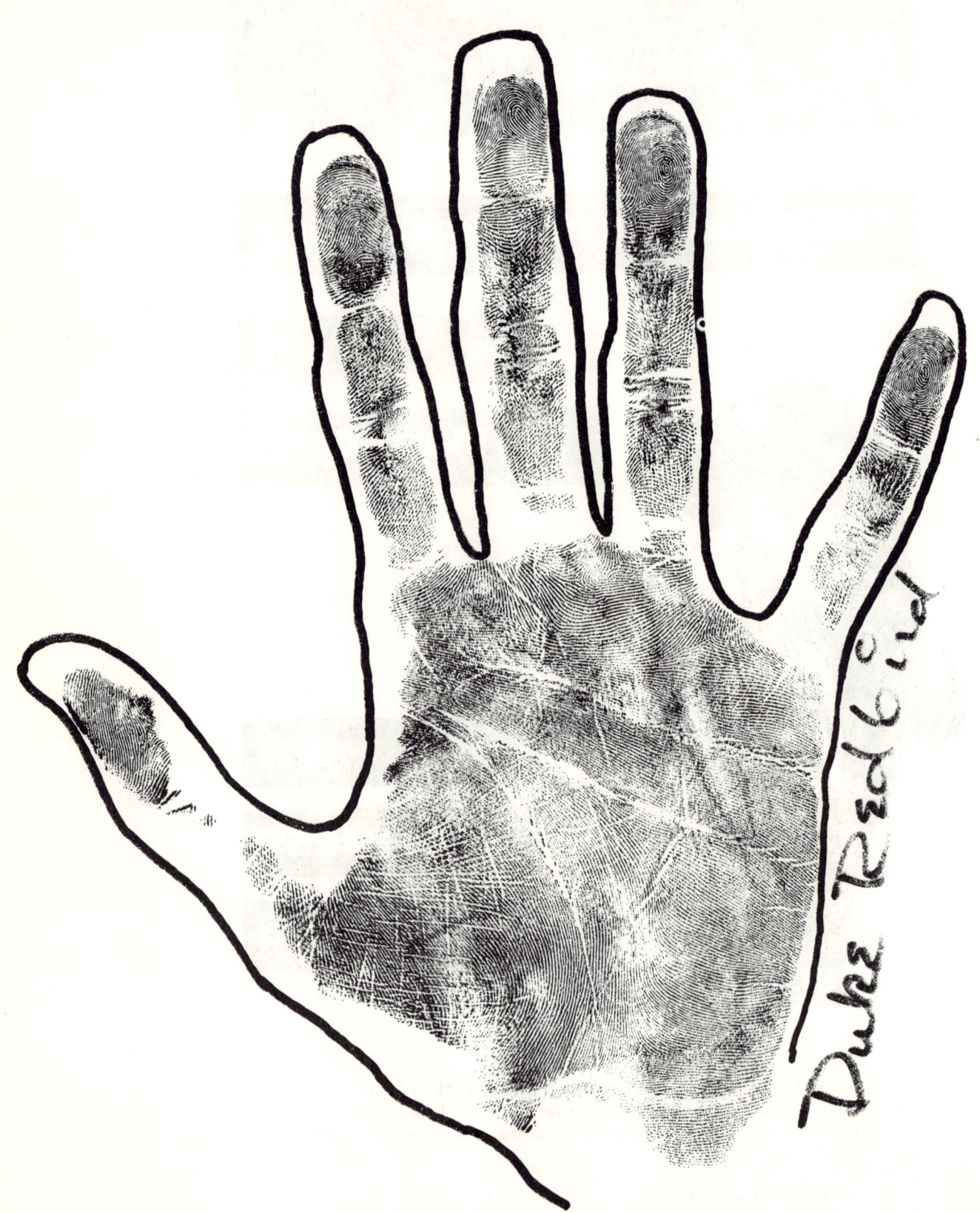

```
xxxxxxxxxxxxxxxxxxxxxxxxxxxxxxxxxxxxxxxxxxxxx
xxxxxxxxxxxxxxxxxxxxxxxxxxxxxxxxxxxxxxxxxxxxx
xxxxxxxxxxxxxxxxxxxxxxxxxxxxxxxxxxxxxxxxxxxxx
xxxxxxxxxxxxxxxxxxxxxxxxxxxxxxxxxxxxxxxxxxxxx
xxxxxxxxxxxxxxxxxxxxxxxxxxxxxxxxxxxxxxxxxxxxx

xxxxxxxxxxxxxxxxxxxxxxxxxxxxxxxxxxxxxxxxxxxxx
xxxxxxxxxxxxxxxxxxxxxxxxxxxxxxxxxxxxxxxxxxxxx
xxxxxxxxxxxxxxxxxxxxxxxxxxxxxxxxxxxxxxxxxxxxx
xxxxxxxxxxxxxxxxxxxxxxxxxxxxxxxxxxxxxxxxxxxxx
xxxxxxxxxxxxxxxxxxxxxxxxxxxxxxxxxxxxxxxxxxxxx
```

I Ching thrown for life space

```
xaxtwofoldxpossibilityxisxpresentedxtoxx
thexgreatxmanxhexcanxsoarxtoxthexheights
andxplayxanximportantxpartxinxthexworldx
xorxhexcanxwithdrawxintoxsolitudexandxxx
xdevelopxhimselfxeachxmustxmakexaxchoice
accordingxtoxthexinnerxlawxofxhisxbeingx

axspherexofxinfluencexopensxupxforxthexx
xgreatxmanxdangerxlurksxatxthexplacexofx
xtransitionxgreatnessxisxnotximpairedxby
temptationsxhexwhoxremainsxinxtouchxwith
xxthextimexthatxisxdawningxxandxwithxits
xxxdemandsxprudentlyxavoidsxallxpitfalls
```

```
xxxxxxxxxxxxxxxxxxxxxxxxxxxxxxxxxxxxxxxxxxxxx
xxxxxxxxxxxxxxxxxxxxxxxxxxxxxxxxxxxxxxxxxxxxx
xxxxxxxxxxxxxxxxxxxxxxxxxxxxxxxxxxxxxxxxxxxxx
xxxxxxxxxxxxxxxxxxxxxxxxxxxxxxxxxxxxxxxxxxxxx
xxxxxxxxxxxxxxxxxxxxxxxxxxxxxxxxxxxxxxxxxxxxx
```

```
xxxninexatxthexbeginningxmeansxhiddenxxx
xxdragonxdoxnotxactxthexdragonxisxthexx
xxxsymbolxofxthexelectricallyxchargedxxx
xdynamicxforcexthatxmanifestsxitselfxinx
xxthexthunderxstormxthisxsymbolizesxaxxx
xxxgreatxmanxwhoxisxstillxunrecognizedxx
```

The Creative

"I myself am a question which is addressed to the world, and I must communicate my answer, for otherwise I am dependent on the world's answer"

C. G. JUNG

I AM THE REDMAN
SON OF THE FOREST, MOUNTAIN, AND LAKE.
    WHAT USE HAVE I OF ASPHALT?
    WHAT USE HAVE I OF BRICK AND CONCRETE?
    WHAT USE HAVE I OF THE AUTOMOBILE?
THINK YOU THESE GIFTS DIVINE,
THAT I SHOULD BE HUMBLY GRATEFUL?

I AM THE REDMAN
SON OF THE TREE, HILL, AND STREAM.
    WHAT USE HAVE I OF CHINA AND CRYSTAL?
    WHAT USE HAVE I OF DIAMONDS AND GOLD?
    WHAT USE HAVE I OF MONEY?
THINK YOU THESE FROM HEAVEN SENT,
THAT I SHOULD BE EAGER TO ACCEPT?

I AM THE REDMAN
SON OF THE EARTH AND WATER AND SKY.
    WHAT USE HAVE I OF SILK AND VELVET?
    WHAT USE HAVE I OF NYLON AND PLASTIC?
    WHAT USE HAVE I OF YOUR RELIGION?
THINK YOU THESE BE HOLY AND SACRED
THAT I SHOULD KNEEL IN AWE?

I AM THE REDMAN
I LOOK AT YOU WHITE BROTHER
AND I SAY TO YOU:
SAVE NOT ME FROM SIN AND EVIL,
SAVE YOURSELF.

"Duke Redbird? Why write a book about him? What the hell did he ever do?"

The more that people asked these questions when I mentioned I was doing a biography of Duke Redbird, the more obvious it became that the only way to answer them was to do the book. Norman Mailer expressed my attitude exactly when he said in an interview with Nathan Cohen a couple of years ago;

"The most interesting people I have met were those who contained within themselves the greatest number of contradictions."

From that point of view, Duke Redbird is worth a library. As a man, as an Indian, even as a Canadian, he has a unique quality, both in his personality and his life style. It is this very quality that makes him loved and hated, respected and reviled—very often all of these by the same people at different times.

To identify Duke you need a catalogue of labels. He is a mystic, a painter, a hypnotist, a businessman, a prophet, a poet, a politician, a writer, a sideshow freak, a lecturer, a playboy, an actor, a red-power militant, a lover, and most recently, an independent television producer. Even this list only begins to describe the roles Duke has played. They are all part of the mosaic of his personality. And that is the determining factor in the structure of this book.

> Indian people are wandering around in an abyss of ignorance because they don't really understand how the world they live in reflects their own personalities. They hang on to some kind of traditional past they don't understand and can't really identify with.

There would be no conventional verbal portrait of Duke that could even come close to communicating the meaning of the man. His incredibly diverse and often spotted career—to say nothing of the mercurial processes of his mind—defy linear description, as he himself defies nineteenth-century linear reality.

He is a man of the new age, an exotic and often frustrating blend of contradictions, enigmas and in the best sense of the word, creativity: for it is out of these very contradictions that his creativity comes. Out of the conflict between his contempt for white society and his need for love and approval came his painting and his poetry. From the conflict between his fantasy mind-world and the cold reality in which he lived, came his militancy and his philosophy. From the synthesis of these conflicts came his concept of the new North American man in the electronic, cybernetic world of the twenty-first century.

To even attempt to communicate this kind of reality, the book itself must be a mosaic: a collection of information, of episodes, of concepts and of images, that weave themselves together to reflect the character and the reality of the man. The mosaic technique is one way of getting between the lines of a conventional biography to portray the reality of a truly unique Canadian.

Another unusual feature of the book is the use of what I call the synchronistic sciences: numerology, palmistry, astrology, the tarot and the I Ching. These are presented without explanation in an attempt to add still another dimension to the portrait of the man.

WHAT SHOULD I DO?—SIT HERE AND TALK ABOUT HOW GREAT THE WHITE MAN IS? GOD KNOWS HE PUBLISHES ENOUGH BOOKS AND DOES ENOUGH OF HIS OWN PUBLIC RELATIONS, TELLING THE WORLD HOW GREAT HE IS. IF HE WANTS TO HEAR HOW GREAT HE IS HE CAN PAY ME A CERTAIN AMOUNT OF MONEY AND THEN MAYBE I'LL GET UP ON A SOAP BOX AND TELL HIM HOW GREAT HE IS; BUT IF HE WANTS TO KNOW THE TRUTH ABOUT WHAT I FEEL, THEN THAT'S A DIFFERENT STORY. WHAT I'M TALKING ABOUT ARE THINGS HE DOESN'T WANT TO HEAR. THE WHITE MAN BLOWS HIS OWN HORN ABOUT HOW GREAT HE IS. I DON'T HAVE TO DO IT FOR HIM. I COULD MAKE SPEECHES ABOUT HOW GREAT HE IS, BUT THERE ARE TWENTY MILLION PEOPLE IN THIS COUNTRY TO DO THAT.

I met Duke eight years ago in Canada's first free school, Yorkville Village. Writers, poets, artists, philosophers, musicians, hustlers, hookers, dealers, freaks and hangers-on were being drawn together by the magic of a community without definitions or rules. We all had two things in common: a desire to escape from middle-class monotony or lower-class poverty and an urge to find or create a new life-style which had more happening than our society offered.

It was in this intense, exciting, hotbed of hope and frustration that Duke found the beginnings of the acceptance he had sought all his life. The first time I saw Duke I was sitting in the then Village Corner patio on Avenue Road. I watched in growing disbelief as a young couple walked toward the club.

The man was tall and slender, in his early twenties. An elk-skin, fringed vest flapped rhythmically around his shirtless chest as he walked and he walked with an arrogance that knew every eye was on him. He wore a pair of tight blue-jeans spattered with multi-hued paint and slit at the calves and the slit fastened with a beaded Thunderbird disk. His hair was black and thick and combed into a sweeping ducksass à la Elvis Presley. He wore the pretty, vixenish woman on his arm like an ornament.

As he stepped into the patio a storm of greeting covered his entrance—and it was an entrance. Everybody seemed to know him, and there was a flurry of hand-shaking, hugging and laughter. Toni Maracle, a Hamilton girl who was managing the patio and much of the village scene at the time, brought him to our table and introduced him.

There was an immediate, if somewhat guarded, rapport between us as we swapped identification information. He was impressed by the fact that I was working as a photographer-reporter for the Tely, and I was intrigued by his brash confidence, quick tongue, alert mind and ready laugh. I had never met anyone quite like him.

I had met many Indians from Walpole Island while working for the Windsor Star, but this was an entirely different breed of cat. He leaped effortlessly from topic to topic, usually steering things into a joke or caustic point, but underneath the banter and the brashness was a fierce intensity, a sense of self or being, that was stronger in him than in anyone I'd met.

He was full of self-important enthusiasm about an Indian fort he was opening next to Honest Ed's discount store and he spun out a yarn about how he walked into Ed Mirvish's office—painted jeans and all—and walked out with a cheque to finance his operations. His stories, jokes and sharp insights into the foibles of the people he'd met kept us entranced far into the early morning.

A few days later I ran into him again and he had a small, but beautifully-formed German shepherd bitch with him, named Kim. Duke and Kim were inseparable. The only time she wasn't with him was when he ordered her to guard his car, and God help anybody who tried to get into the car without Duke. She obeyed his every whim, as he proved once by ordering her to eat a dill pickle.

As the bond between Duke and me grew stronger, his bitterness and anger at the white world around him became more evident. He seemed amazed that I would admit Indian ancestry when there was nothing in my appearance to give it away. At the same time, there was a growing pride in his own Indian identity.

Indian people often ask me what the difference is between the red and the white race. They read in the newspapers that there is no difference, but I don't believe that. I simply ask them if there is any difference between the people sitting in that very room. I only have to point out that there are men and women in the room, and they begin to see what kind of difference exists.

During the next year I was drawn into the Redbird scene. We had a series of adventures and misadventures which are best left to the book proper, but in that time the contradictions contained in this one personality became even more obvious.

As the months went by, his Indian identity syndrome became more and more aggressive. His contact with the newly-formed National Indian Council resulted in his becoming editor of the controversial and short-lived Thunderbird newspaper—Canada's first National Indian newspaper. He became more absorbed by the idea of red power, though nobody was calling it that in those days.

At the other end of the spectrum he frequently got drunk, and cliche or not, this Indian and alcohol just don't mix. One night he sat, drunk, in the middle of the floor of an unused coach house. Tears were streaming down his face and he was ripping at his face with his fingernails, shouting that he wanted to tear everything Indian out of himself. That night finished with him sitting cross-legged in a self-induced hypnotic trance chanting:

The rest of the story I'll leave to the book. The book itself, by the way, could never have been created without the loving help of Margaret Laurence and her hours of taped interviews with Duke, or without the patience and interviews of **new press** publisher Jim Bacque who lived in suspense for more than a year, wondering if his brain-child would ever be born. Special thanks too, to Alec Bruyns, a freelance photographer whose creative techniques made the illustrations and collages possible.

Along this life's highway
Are many dwellings.
Some are distant, with long rocky pathways to their doors,
Others are close, their warmth beckons for you to call.
One day as I was walking
Along life's uncertain highway
I chanced to see a dwelling
At whose door I wished to call.
It sat high upon a distant hill,
So imposing and so alone,
That I felt it needed someone
To whom it could become a home.
I turned from my uncertain travel
Along life's fleeting highway
And walked the rocky pathway
To that house upon the hill.
My heart was light, my eyes were bright, and,
I thought, "I'll stop here a moment to catch my breath.
Then, when evening comes
I'll find my way to shelter with those walls so strong and warm."
The sun was down when I arrived. The long dark shadows
Of the night were dancing at my feet.
I tried the door; it was bolted from the inside.
"Let me in.
I'm a stranger from the highway
And I would pause a moment 'till the morning light can guide
Me on my way."

"Go away," a voice replied,
"I can't unbolt the door.
For another whom I do not know, and haven't met has the key
And is the rightful owner."

    "But I only wish to stop a while, 'till the passing of night's
                                                                dark clouds.
    I'll not disturb your house."

"Go away," the voice replied,
"Can't you see
That I'm happy here inside
And I'm not the kind
Whose door is open wide
To any stranger who passes by?
But you are a stranger
And I do not wish to provide a situation that might be dangerous
To the perfect order of my house.
For I'm most happy when I'm alone.
And there are others I have known
And I would not give them shelter either."

    It was no use, and I turned away,
    And I heard the voice say;

"Do not be angry.
You must understand.

I do not mind if you stand out there and talk to me.
I'd surely enjoy your company."

    I smiled as the voice faded into the night,
    And I returned to the highway
    And wondered: when the rightful owner came,
    Would he be received the same? . . . . . .

Aquarian Tarot

Gary James Richardson was born March 18, 1939, in an old farmhouse on the Saugeen Reserve on the Bruce Peninsula, near Owen Sound. His father, Big Jack Richardson, an Irish-Indian, joked with the doctor about his son missing St. Patrick's day, while his mother, Kathleen, gave birth to her sixth and last child.

Like many Canadian Indians, the Richardson family followed work around the country to support themselves. Shortly after Gary's birth, they moved into a small shack outside St. Catharines, where Big Jack worked in the orchards. Accustomed to making do with whatever facilities were available, the family turned the shack into a home for the season.

Duke was just nine months old, when one day, a leg on an old wood-burning stove in the shack gave way. The stove toppled, throwing flaming coals into the tiny room. With the single doorway blocked by flames, Mrs. Richardson frantically shepherded her four older children through a window. She threw a pillow out into the snow and dropped her baby to safety.

Too big to get through the window herself, she ran to the door, through the flames. John, the oldest brother, remembers his mother coming through the door, her skin bursting with blisters. She died the next day in the hospital.

Deserted himself as a child, by his unmarried mother, Big Jack Richardson had carved a bare existence out of the unfriendly world around him. Unable to cope with his fight for survival and the responsibility of raising five children, he turned his family over to the Children's Aid Society foster care program.

> Here is a guy who doesn't have anything. He has a wife whom he loves and five children. One day his whole world collapses. His house burns down. His wife is burned up in the fire. And he is left with five children, no money and very little to offer but his own strength. He told me he took a walk across a bridge and stood for a long time wondering if he should jump off or face it. If I had been in the same circumstances, would I have had the strength to face it? I'm sure he didn't want to lose us, but what could he do for us? As it turned out, he was looking ahead for my best interests. When I realized that was what he had done, I learned to love and respect him

The Society's social workers arranged for overnight care for the children the day of the fire and Duke was taken to the home of Mr. and Mrs. Walter Jukes in St. Catharines.

Mrs. Jukes remembers that the original proposal was to keep the child for a day or two, but she formed a strong attachment for the infant and agreed to keep him indefinitely.

For the next six years Gary lived as a white child in the white middle-class world of the Jukes and their two sons, Bill and Ernie. The chunky, rough-and-ready, multi-talented Walter Jukes and his ambitious, driving, status-conscious wife were, as far as Gary was concerned, his mother and father. Gary loved his home.

But even this illusion was shattered, when Gary, then six, overheard a conversation between his foster father and the family doctor.

I like the boy very much but I'm afraid we'll have to get rid of him.

Gary, too young and too afraid to ask questions, didn't want to know any more, but the words burned into his mind and seared his whole reality. He was different; he didn't really belong. He was alone.

Gary had been told by his foster parents that he was an Indian—but until he overheard that conversation, it didn't mean anything to him. Now he sensed that it was something that made him unwanted, that separated him from people, even those he thought were his mother and father. His fear that being an Indian was some kind of handicap was intensified when he started school that fall at Consolidated Public School in St. Catharines. He was the only Indian in the school.

> My school-mates chanted "Cowboys and Itchybums" It didn't take long to figure out who the Itchybum was

Uncomfortable at home, an Itchybum at school, Gary fled into his fantasy world. He fought, and often, when he had to, but he kept the battles to himself. His dislike of competitive sports alienated him from his classmates even more, but he discovered he could draw.

He liked to draw and he drew constantly, filling his notebooks with caricatures and daydreams. A few teachers encouraged and praised his work, which was for Gary his only source of approval. But other teachers were quick to impose conventions. One day he was handed a mimeographed picture of a child in a snowsuit to colour. He coloured the pants purple and the top blue, and the teacher was quick to point out that he couldn't mix colours like that. It looked alright to Gary, but he accepted the criticism.

Gary's sense of being different from everyone he knew became acute three years later, when his father, Big Jack Richardson, bought a house down the street from the Jukes' place. He moved in with his woman and Gary's brother and three sisters. The move scandalized the neighborhood, and Gary was warned to have nothing to do with them. He was forbidden even to speak to them.

I feel my mother was sacrificed, to get me where I am now I have a responsibility to that sacrifice

All my memories of that period have to do with being sad, being scared, being in a state of nervous tension. The only time I could get away from that was when I was alone and could use my imagination to create a world that had some peace and serenity. I was always searching for my mother. I thought that if my mother were alive, she wouldn't let all these bad things happen to me. Sometimes I would have a sense of her being near me. I could never rationalize out in my head the reasons I couldn't have a normal childhood and a mother and father and people that loved me. As a kid, I never felt love. I got approval when things I did were right, and disapproval most of the time—because everything I did seemed to be wrong—but never love. It was something I really wanted. In my fantasy world I spent a lot of time imagining myself in a position of power—power over my life—power to be happy—but never experiencing this sort of power.

For the next three years, Gary went to the same school as his brother and sisters—but lived in an entirely different world. A fence was put up at the rear of the Jukes' property. Gary stayed on one side, his family on the other. He silently absorbed another confusing lesson about what it meant to be a Canadian Indian.

There I was, marching off to school in new clothes and new shoes while my brother, who lived only a few doors away, had to wear tattered clothes and shoes with holes in them. Somehow I knew they were from the other side of the tracks, and I really didn't want to have anything to do with them. My brother hated me for that.

Gary was called Jukes at school, then it changed to Dukes and then to Duke. He readily accepted the name and the peculiar kind of status that went with it. Duke was learning that there were advantages to being different. He was learning to cope with the people around him. He learned to read the moods of his foster parents and teachers and to keep his best side toward them. He applied his new knowledge to his friends as well.

Duke was discovering that there were a lot of other people on the "outside" of the world he found himself in. By aligning himself with these people—usually the rough-tough guys in the class—he eliminated most of the friction with the cowboys and itchybums faction. He was finding out that fear works almost as well as friendship when it comes to manipulating people.

At home, his relationship with his foster father was changing. Walter Jukes, harried by his immediate family, turned to the affection-hungry orphan for comfort. Duke was an avid listener for Jukes' stories of his rough-and-tumble days in the boxing world. Together they explored the woods, on the property Walter Jukes had bought in the Kawartha Lakes region of Northern Ontario.

Despite fierce and continued opposition from Mrs. Jukes, Walter gave Duke his first twenty-two rifle. He taught Duke to track small game and to find his way safely through dense bush. Away from the bitter conflicts of home and the social intrigues of a white classroom, the pair found a sense of peace in the woods. And Duke's foster father was quick to praise his growing skill in the bush and his ability to bag small game.

Up to now, Duke's fantasy world had been his own, but he discovered that others, less imaginative, were more than willing to play his games and enter his fantasy world. In this fantasy world he was Clark Kent who allowed himself to be meek with others, but alone—when the magic words were spoken—he took on his super identity.

He had already learned that the line between truth and fantasy is non-existent. His own experience taught him that there was much more to reality than most people were willing to talk about to an eight-year-old.

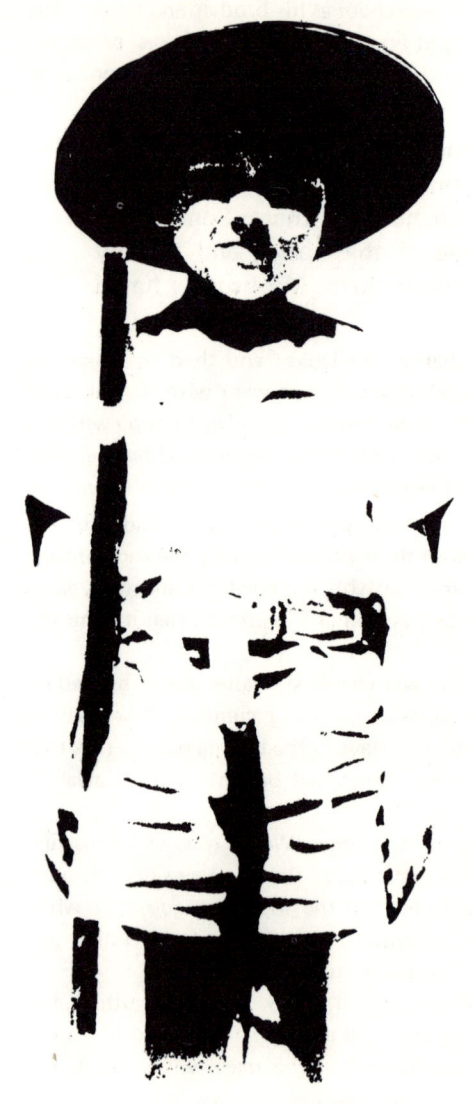

I was forever building forts: tree forts, and forts in the bush. In these forts I was always the leader, the commander, the organizer. There was a real gang of us; we had this fantasy that someday the Germans would come and we had our fort and we would somehow defeat them.

I was in my bedroom. I was not asleep, or really awake, but the dream—or vision if you want to call it that—is as clear now as the day it happened. I saw the ceiling of my room dissolve, and in the vacuum, a silver cloud appeared on which three men in white robes were standing. In the midst of these three men stood a silver cross. The men did not speak to me, but I knew they were aware of me, and this gave me great comfort. It still does.

In the Jukes' home, Duke found himself in a marital no-man's land. His foster father escaped into alcohol, and Duke sought the company of his street cronies more often, as his foster mother became more demanding. The Jukes wouldn't speak for weeks on end, and Duke delivered messages between them in these periods of intense conflict.

Walter Jukes died of a stroke when Duke was eleven years old. The family was at the camp in the Kawartha Lakes, and for Duke, it was a long, dark, frightening night.

My mom, Walter and myself, were the only ones in the cabin at the time. Walter collapsed and mom sent me out to the neighbors' for help. It was in the middle of night and so black you really couldn't see your hand in front of your face. I got to the neighbors' and banged and banged on the door. I knew that he was in serious trouble and had to get help. By the time I got back to the house he was in very bad pain. I couldn't understand what was happening. The neighbors came and put a mattress in the back of a pick-up truck and drove him the forty miles to hospital, but he was dead when they got there.

This was the first time anybody who was close to me had died. I had to face up to the fact that people died. I wasn't quite sure what was going to happen after that, but I knew things would change drastically—and they did.

As Duke put it, the vultures descended. The rest of the family began to pressure Mrs. Jukes to get rid of Duke. Mrs. Jukes, suffering from nervous tension, blamed worry over Duke for an outbreak of hives and told him that the neighbors were saying that she had been to bed with some Indian passing through town.

Duke aggravated the situation by his escapades away from home. Now in grade eight, Duke had a new friend: an outsider and a thirteen-year-old graduate from several reform schools, John Smythe. He and Duke sneaked out of their homes at night and wandered the streets until the early hours of the morning. Anything Smythe wanted he stole, and he was an expert at small-change operations like newspaper boxes and telephone booths. Duke served as a look-out.

Towards the end of the school year, Smythe was sent back to the reformatory, but Duke had had a taste of street life, and had picked up a few angles for making money, and with money, being an Indian didn't seem to matter so much.

Duke started badly at Meritton High School in St. Catharines. History and art were the only subjects that interested him and he simply ignored the rest. To finance his

My foster mother was going through a difficult period then, a period of terrible nervous strain, and she had a terrible, terrible temper. But now she's almost seventy and she's a very beautiful person. She operates the Jukes' camp in the Kawartha Lakes and she's still capable of taking off into the bush with a rifle. She loves to eat partridge.

I thought it was a grand house. It was designed and built by Walter Jukes in the Spanish bungalow style. It had two willow trees in front and this white picket fence all around the property.

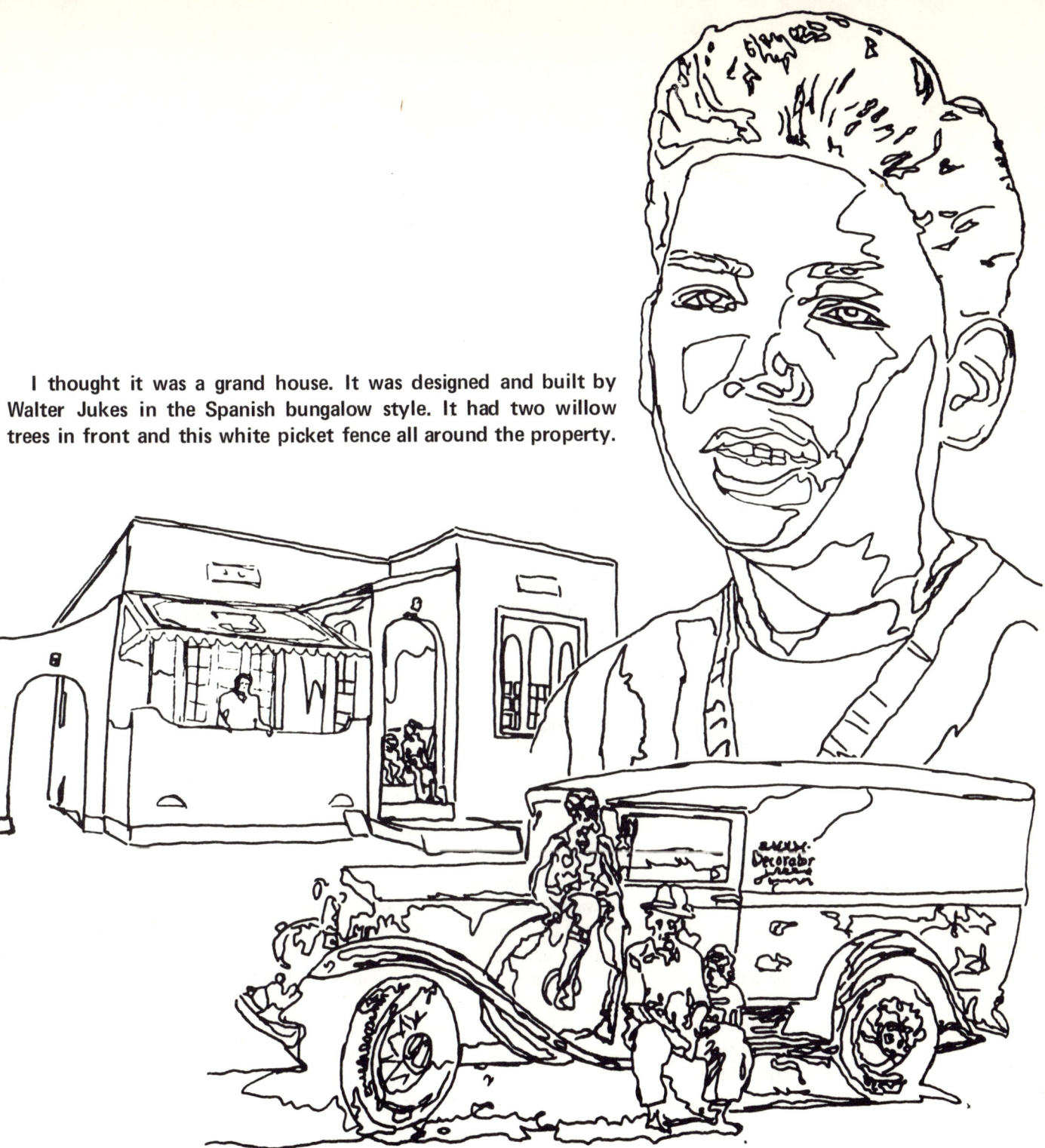

rapidly growing social life, he drew nude pictures of the prettiest girls in class and sold them to the other boys for a quarter.

Using some hypodermic needles that Smythe had provided, Duke spiked oranges with vodka supplied by a local rubby; these, he sold for a dollar apiece. He spent a lot of time with girl friends, and more time thinking about getting out of school.

Mrs. Jukes was terrified by the things that were happening. She simply couldn't handle the growing rebellion in Duke and was convinced by the rest of the family that Duke was going to sully the Jukes' name. That summer she told him he was "going to visit" someplace else.

Duke sensed that it would be more than a "visit." He packed his bags on the final day and carried them to the back porch. They waited for the social worker from the Children's Aid without speaking. There was little left to be said.

It hurt me to leave, but by this time I was feeling pretty independent. I felt I could take care of myself. I didn't need anybody. I had a burning desire to prove that I was more than they made me out to be. I didn't want to stay in school and become a reasonable facsimile of what they thought I should be. If it had been up to the Jukes, I'm sure I would have been in some kind of trade—but I knew I was more gifted than that.

Everytime I did something wrong, I was told I was acting like a Richardson—that the Richardson was coming out in me—that it was a bad thing I had to fight all the time to be worth-while. When the Jukes' family decided I couldn't carry their name any more—it might have hurt the business—I figured, O.K., I'll be a Richardson. If I've got the name I might as well have the game. So I did all the bad things I was told Richardsons were supposed to do.

With the social worker, Duke travelled to Chippawa, near Niagara Falls, to the working-class home of Bill and Jean Hodge. He was treated like a visitor in their home, and that was just the way he wanted it. He kept to himself as much as he could. He was repeating grade nine at Stamford Collegiate, but was spending more time in pool halls than at school. He had changed his name to Richardson.

Duke and a friend, Bob, "Jesse" James, began to take short hitch-hiking trips to St. Thomas, London, and north to the bush country. The freedom of the road lured him more and more as the year wore on, but that summer, his foster brother Ernie got him a job in the press room of Border Advertising services. For thirty dollars a week, Duke discovered labour.

THAT JOB TAUGHT ME ONE THING; I DIDN'T WANT TO WORK LIKE THAT FOR THE REST OF MY LIFE. I KNEW I HAD TO STAY IN SCHOOL.

When the school year started again, Duke wasn't welcome at the Hodge home. He moved into an attic with two friends who lived by stealing, and hustling homosexuals. Duke went back to school, raked leaves for money and bummed food from other kids at school.

By comparison, his life with the Jukes had been idyllic. In letters written at the time to Mrs. Jukes, he remembers the happiness they had shared, and he signed himself, "your prodical (sic) son." He suggested that it would be nice to be back with them. Ernie, himself married, and establishing an advertising agency, offered his home to Duke. Duke moved back to St. Catharines and continued grade ten.

With his wordly airs, his growing flair for sparking things into action, and his habit of connecting himself to the prettiest girls in school, Duke was swept up into high school social life, but the upper-middle-class students had clothes, money and cars, and Duke just couldn't keep up.

His interest in school fell off, in exact proportion to his decline in status. With a pool hall buddy, Cliff Spears, he decided to quit in the spring. Before he left his foster brother's home, he had a visit from his father.

WHILE I WAS IN MY LAST FOSTER HOME, MY FATHER DROVE UP IN AN OLD 1939 PLYMOUTH WITH THE BACK SEAT TORN OUT. HE HAD SOME OLD BOXES IN THERE AND HE HAD MY SISTER SHERRI WITH HIM. HE LOOKED LIKE SOMETHING THAT HAD JUST COME OUT OF THE OZARKS. HE WAS A TALL MAN AND HE ALWAYS WORE THIS FUNNY STOCK HAT. I WAS GLAD TO SEE HIM, BUT A BIT ASHAMED. I WOULD RATHER HAVE SEEN HIM DRIVE UP IN A BIG CADILLAC, WITH LOTS OF MONEY. HE WAS A POOR MAN MATERIALLY, BUT RICH IN A PERSONAL, SPIRITUAL WAY. BUT I HAD NO WAY OF KNOWING THAT AT THE TIME.

With school behind him, and the ties with his foster family all but severed, Duke found himself without roots and with no visible future. He was restless and hungry for meaning, for identification in the world around him. Instinctively, he began searching for his real family, hoping that with them he would find some place where he really belonged. In his fantasies he imagined them as rich people who would be glad to see him and would love and take care of him.

He began with a search for his brother. Wearing his only suit, a blue gabardine, and with fifty cents in his pocket, he thumbed his way to Buffalo where he'd heard his brother was living. Being an Indian, he was able under the Jay Treaty to cross the border without visible means of support. He was to take advantage of this particular treaty provision again later. Once in Buffalo, he was directed to his brother's address.

> His place was a terrible slum. My brother's wife, Dorothy, let me in and I waited for John to come home. She met him at the door and told him I was there, and I heard him say, "What the hell does he want?" We got to talking and became pals and he took me out and showed me around Buffalo.
>
> I was hoping my brother would be very well-off. I was going to discover my family and all that. But he was an artist and on the brink of starvation. He had all kinds of trouble of his own, and I was just another problem for him. So I left.

Duke went back to St. Catharines and moved in with Cliff Spears and his family. He worked in a shoe store for three weeks, and then quit for a job erecting tents in an army camp, at Niagara-on-the-Lake. He worked hard and was soon straw boss of his group and later—as a reward—was made an officer's orderly. All he had to do was look busy, and with fifty-five dollars a week in his pocket, Duke made the most of it.

Duke and Cliff bought black leather jackets, heavy black boots, black jeans, and black shirts. The idea caught on with nearly fifty of the army work-gang. The pair emerged as leaders of a street gang: Cliff because he was tough enough to take on any of them, and Duke because he knew how to use his head.

Duke named the gang the Tyrants, created their symbol of a spider on a skull, and began carrying a knife. The gang was forever planning small-time break-ins, but Duke found a way around it.

We were like a motorcycle gang without motorcycles—we had cars. As soon as somebody came up with an idea for a small job, we immediately launched these great plans for knocking over something big—like the steel company. We would draw up these intricate plans for timing the guards and so on, and by the time we got into it, it was so complicated everybody was glad to drop the idea.

In between plans for robbing banks, Duke drove a truck for a fur company and washed rugs in a factory, that is until Cliff was fired for drinking on the job. It was Christmas, they were bored, and they had no money.

Friends were drifting into St. Catharines with fat bank rolls and wild stories of the life in the mining camps at Elliot Lake. It took no more than that to put Duke, Cliff and a third friend, Andy Stokes, on the road to fortune.

With twenty dollars among them, and all they owned packed into a suitcase, they thumbed their way to North Bay. They stayed in a hotel overnight, then pushed on to Sudbury, penniless. In Sudbury, they were told that they should have been hired in Toronto, but that there was a catering firm that might take them on. They split up for the night to make it easier to find places to sleep. Duke sat in a restaurant for hours to escape the bitter cold. Finally he was asked to leave.

It was two o'clock in the morning, twenty below zero, and Duke had no place to go. To keep warm, he started running through the streets. He ran and ran, for three hours. Then, exhausted and confused, he simply lay down in the street.

A short while later, a nameless immigrant forced him to his feet and rubbed his body, face and hands to get his circulation moving. The man took him to the local YMCA where the desk clerk agreed to let him sleep in the hall until the morning shift came on.

The next day he met his friends in the railway station and they signed on with the catering company as bull cooks, or janitors. They worked at their jobs during the day, and at night Duke hustled extra money by acting as a runner for local poker games. The job ended suddenly when Duke got into an argument with an office worker who had the seniority to demand Duke's room. Duke was fired and back on the road.

Duke and Andy decided to head for Vancouver, via the United States. They hitch-hiked to Sault Ste. Marie, Michigan and were headed for the International Falls, when they were pulled over by a sheriff. They were frisked for guns, questioned and driven off to jail. They moped in the jail for two days and were finally questioned by the border patrol and delivered to the ferry for Sault Ste. Marie, Canada.

Once on the Canadian side, Andy split for home, and Duke stayed on at a local flop house. He learned from the rubbies where he could get food and shelter for a few nights at a time. His first stop was the police station, where he shovelled coal for a few hours to earn a meal ticket. He heard of an accountant, a Gideon, who fed people in return for listening to bible lectures. Duke ate and listened.

Finally he tried the unemployment office, and got a job as an extra on the railway gang. There had been a severe snow storm and they were hiring people to clear the tracks. Duke showed up early to cash in on a free breakfast.

Without overshoes or gloves, Duke walked three miles to a tool shed for shovels, and started working on clearing the switches. He had worked for ninety minutes when a foreman spotted him without gloves and fired him. He was afraid that Duke's hands would freeze and that the railway would be liable. Duke headed for St. Catharines without picking up his time.

The first flush of freedom that Duke had felt on leaving school had paled to confusion. Once again he turned to his family as a contact with reality. He heard his father had just bought some land in Carlyle, Ontario, and decided to join this strange man he knew so little and needed so much. With his father, he discovered a new world, a world where middle-class values simply didn't exist. He became part of a new way of life, and began to learn what kind of man his father was.

The connection between the two was unique, and objective narrative threatens to destroy its flavour. The only way the story can effectively be told is in Duke's own words.

My father had this way about him when he walked into a place. He had a style about him, like: "Well, here I am, Big Jack, King of the World." which I thought, at first, was ridiculous because he didn't have the outward trappings of a man that walked around with that much confidence and pride.

As far as I know, he was the illegitimate son of an Indian woman and a medical student, in a place called Bracebridge. He was abandoned at five or six by his mother and picked up by a carnival passing through town. I'm not sure how he acquired the name Richardson. It was just a name he picked up along the way.

He travelled with the carnival until he was about fifteen and never went to school, though he taught himself to read and write. He had a lot of knowledge about a lot of different things; you name it and he knew something about it. He worked at all kinds of different jobs—everything from a deputy Texas Ranger to a streetcar-driver in St. Louis.

He was constantly putting everybody on by his grouchiness. He acted like a man who didn't like children or dogs—almost like W. C. Fields, but not quite as harsh. He always had this twinkle in his eye. He made me feel that if I wanted to be in his league I couldn't be a person who felt sorry for myself, or have any troubles. To be in his league you had to have a smile about you, and take everything with a grain of salt, and be a happy, humorous kind of individual. He was the kind of man who was happy with what life had brought him, even if he wasn't successful.

He never gave me a Christmas present or a birthday present, which used to bother me. I found out later, that at

Christmas-time he used to make a batch of candy-apples, and take them to Sick Kids' Hospital and hand them out to the kids: but to his own kids he wouldn't show that kind of affection. It was like he was saying, "You help other people, but for yourself, you have to be stronger and above that."

It used to bother me that I didn't have anything to go and show other people that he'd done for me. I sensed that he was proud of me and that he liked me. He wasn't a particularly kind father, but he would compliment me to other people and I'd hear about it from them later.

When I went to live with him, he was in a little place called Carlyle, just outside of Waterdown, near Hamilton. He had bought some property, an acre or two of land, and he set about building himself a little shack. Now this place wasn't more than about twelve feet long and eight or ten feet wide—just a shack made out of old boards and tin. It was well put-together, warm in the wintertime and so on, but just a shack.

He had a bed in this room, a stove in the middle, a table, a couch and two little windows. He would walk into that place and sit down on the couch and talk about that couch like it was the living room. He would walk over to what he called the kitchen—which was the stove, about three feet away—put on the kettle in the kitchen and make tea in the dining room, which was two feet away on the table. He talked about the house like it was a big mansion, and it was all in one little room.

Coming as I did, as a child, from a middle-class Spanish bungalow, this was difficult for me to accept. He would sit on an old box and call it a chair, and then later he'd tell me to get something from that box. First it was a chair, and now it's a box. His ability to do this was just fascinating, and it made me think that at times my father was not all that realistic. But it wasn't long before I was calling one corner the kitchen and the other corner the living room and so on.

He was working as an operator in a quarry in Waterdown, but he had half-a-

It was a nice feeling when I travelled around with him. He would introduce me to people and say, "This is my son." He actually meant it and it was the truth, and it had never been the truth with any other human being.

dozen trades, at least. He was continually getting calls from all over Ontario as a dynamiter. He was the guy who would go up and put a hole in the right place to blow up a mountain, so that the rocks would all come down where they were supposed to, and all that. On top of that, he was a candy maker. He made salt-water taffy, and peanut-brittle and candy-apples and candy-floss. He had these funny little recipes for making candy with a very special taste. People would come back to the fairs year after year to buy candy from him. He continually amazed me with all the things he could do well. He didn't talk about his talents very much. Somebody would want something done and suddenly he was the expert who could do it.

He had been married, I don't know how many times—and this was another thing about the old man—his love affairs. I met I don't know how many women, who were in love with him and continued to love him, even when he was no longer around. I think he was married five times, and my mother was the only one who bore him any children, and the one he stayed with the longest. After she died there was always a new woman in his life. As old as he was, he was always turning on young girls. I used to be embarrassed out of my mind, because I would go into a restaurant with him and the waitress would get all fascinated with him. And he was fifty-five or fifty-six.

He didn't drink and he didn't gamble. He would go and sit in a beer-parlour and talk with people and have a great time—all on one beer: but you see, he was king of that little group of people.

The thing that impressed me most about him, was that he was never beaten.

As many failures as he had, he never thought about them. He was always after something new. My dad always exaggerated everything; everything was bigger than life. He would lose all his money one day, and wake up with a great new idea and start a whole series of events so he could do what he wanted to do: but he didn't have the resources or the information to do it properly, so it was always a half-assed attempt at success.

Even at sixty years of age—the year he died—he had this fantastic scheme for making a million dollars. He was into popcorn—somehow or other he had bought this franchise from this guy. He had the machines and the bags and things and he was going to put out "Pop's Popcorn." He was going to market it in theatres and so on, right across the country, but an ulcer burst in his stomach and he was taken to hospital.

I was in Welland at the time, forty miles away. A cop knocked on the door and said, "I have some bad news for you. Your father has died." Just like that. Dorothy, my wife, and I put on our coats and walked out to the highway and started hitch-hiking. We got to Jordan, just outside St. Catharines, and there we were at three o'clock in the morning—few cars were coming and those that did, didn't stop. Finally a police car came along and flagged down the next car and explained there was a family emergency and we got a ride right into Hamilton. We stayed at my sister's place and I went to the funeral the next day. I didn't want to go, but I did. I looked at him, and there he was. He was dead; that was that. I've never gone back to Bracebridge, where he died.

When he was in the hospital he was saying things like—"No matter if I'm going to die. I lived a great life and I'm happy that I did it." He was in the hospital bed joking about it with my sisters and telling them not be unhappy because he was going to see their mother on the other side. He had some kind of dream that they were waiting for him over there, and he was ready to go. This was a whole enterprise for him, this business of dying. He was all excited about this new adventure he was getting into.

In the summer of 1957, Duke's father set up a kiddy ride in La Salle Park, Burlington, and turned it over to Duke. He charged ten cents a ride, and even after paying a nut, or rent, of twenty-five percent, he was taking home up to one hundred and fifty dollars a week. He bought a 1950 blue Dodge convertible. He was home with his family, and felt for the first time in his life that he had established a permanent relationship.

Duke noticed a young girl visiting the park every day. She was tall, dark-haired, dark-eyed and beautiful. They began talking and he learned that she was a Mohawk Indian, and very much attracted to him. They dated and, after a few weeks, made love—a first for Duke. In September he married Dorothy May Green.

When the rides closed in the fall, Duke couldn't find work. With nowhere to go, the young couple moved in with Dorothy's parents in Aldershot, near Hamilton. For the first time, Duke found himself living with an Indian family as an Indian. He discovered that the poverty-stricken Canadian Indian had a way of life that was totally unlike anything he had experienced with the white middle-class and working-class families he had lived with.

> It was really a terrible winter and we were all incredibly poor. We ate bannock mostly, which is flour and water and white beans baked on a pan. Once in a while we'd have horse meat, which we could get for ten cents a pound. But the funny thing is, it didn't seem to bother anybody.

THE UNIVERSE IS MY CHURCH,
AND THE EARTH IS ITS ALTAR.
UPON THIS ALTAR I LAY MY SOUL
AND TASTE THE WINE OF GOD'S SACRAMENTS,
AND REPLENISH MY SPIRIT FROM ITS LARDER.

ALL PEOPLE OCCUPY THE PEWS OF THIS CHURCH.
THE SUN AND MOON ARE THIS CHURCH'S VESTMENTS,
WHICH CLOAK ALL NATIONS WITH THEIR RADIANCE.
THE PANORAMA OF LIFE ITSELF IS ITS CEREMONY
AND THE CHANTING DISPENSATIONS ARE ITS RITUAL.

THERE ARE NO PRIESTS IN THIS CHURCH FOR GOD
                                            HIMSELF PRESIDES,
AND EACH INDIVIDUAL HAS THE POWER FOR PROPHECY.
ALL TONGUES SING THE JOYS OF THIS CHURCH,
AND ALL VOICES ARE HEARD.
THERE IS NO SPACE THAT THE HEART OF MANKIND
                                            CANNOT FILL,
NOR ANY CORNER OF HUMAN FULFILLMENT
THAT CANNOT EXPRESS ITS TRUTH IN THIS CHURCH.

THIS CHURCH IS ONENESS AND ETERNAL LIFE WITHOUT
                                            END,
LOVE WITHOUT RESTRICTION, SPIRITUALITY WITHOUT
                                            BOUNDARIES.
IT IS A CREATION SO PURE IT NEED NOT CREATE,
BUT RATHER IT BASKS IN THE ESSENCE OF ITS OWN
                                            ENLIGHTENMENT.

The house itself was a little shack about twenty feet long and ten feet wide. It had a small kitchen and a living room and two very small bedrooms. In that house four families lived—a total of fifteen people, including six kids. We all lived in that little shack without arguments, without a fight, and without money.

There were all kinds of basic differences from other places I had lived in. There was a kind of privacy simply because everybody minded their own business. Nobody was asking you what you were doing or what you were thinking. There was nowhere in the house where somebody could say, "This is my place." In the winter, we all slept in one bed, clothes and all, just to keep warm. Nobody complained about it or blamed anybody else.

During that winter, two Mormon missionaries visited the house. Duke was intrigued by their idea that North American Indians were the Lost Tribe of Israel. They were invited back, and both Dorothy and Duke began visiting the Church of the Latter Day Saints on Hamilton Mountain.

I was searching for something. I was wide-open for some kind of security that things are operating because God or somebody knows the answers. I thought if I could find out exactly what it was, I could be connected to it and be saved.

Brother Tustain, an elder of the church, took Duke aside one day and told him of a dream he had had. In this dream, he saw thousands of people being led to baptism by Duke. The elder wasn't convinced that these people were being baptized into the church, but both were impressed by the intense symbolism of the dream. Duke couldn't help but think of his childhood friends on the silver cloud. Duke and Dorothy were baptized into the church.

At the time, it made sense to Duke to put himself in God's hands, as the elders put it, and he attended services with Dorothy every week. Duke became a member of the Aaronic priesthood, served as a functionary in the church, and gave regular testimony.

They moved to St. Thomas with Brother Tustain and stayed with him until spring. By then, the couple, who were the only Indians in the congregation, had become disillusioned with the church and decided to drop the whole thing.

I LEARNED THAT THE RELIGIOUS WHITES WERE A GROUP OF SUPERIOR SELF-RIGHTEOUS HYPOCRITES. FOR ALL THEIR PRAYING AND PREACHING, THEY WERE, IN REALITY, A LOT OF SCARED PEOPLE WHO COULDN'T COPE WITH THEMSELVES OR WITH LIFE WITHOUT SOMEBODY DIRECTING THEIR LIVES FOR THEM. WHITES ARE A PERFECT PEOPLE FOR A TOTALITARIAN GOVERNMENT. THEY NEED RULES AND REGULATIONS AND DON'T THINK VERY MUCH FOR THEMSELVES.

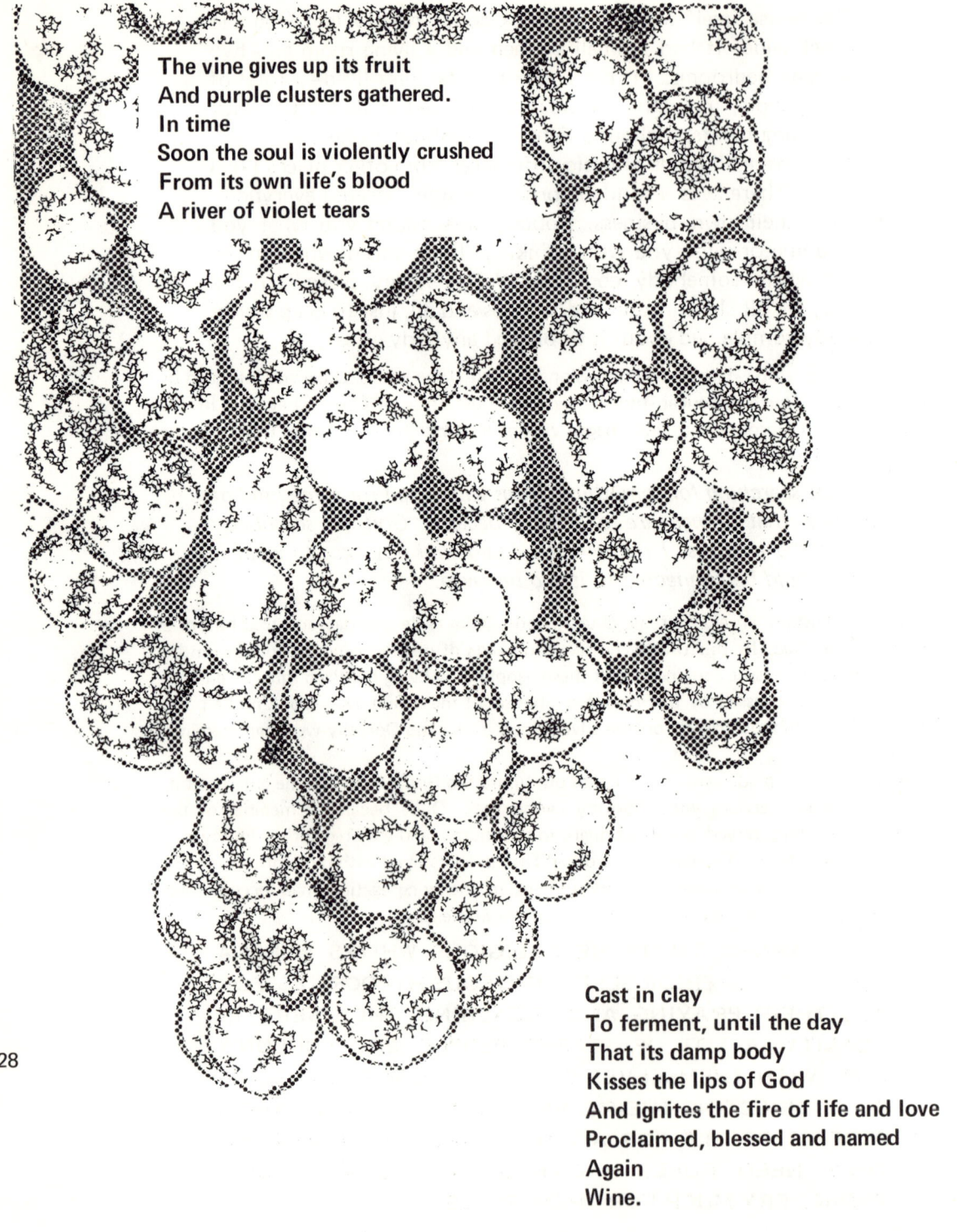

The vine gives up its fruit
And purple clusters gathered.
In time
Soon the soul is violently crushed
From its own life's blood
A river of violet tears

Cast in clay
To ferment, until the day
That its damp body
Kisses the lips of God
And ignites the fire of life and love
Proclaimed, blessed and named
Again
Wine.

Duke stumbled onto one of the few books that up to then, had influenced him; it was The Search for Bridey Murphy. The idea of hypnotism fascinated him and he lost little time in learning the techniques and putting them to use. At first it was a fun thing, but it soon developed into one of Duke's first serious pursuits.

I told so many lies about this trip that I almost forget what the truth is. The reason I told the lies was that it was easier to say something offhand about it than to get into how it really started.

I had always considered that hypnosis was some kind of magic—mysterious and mystical. It was good to keep this idea actually, because it helped to put someone into trance. What I learned about hypnosis though, was that it was a scientific, logical, human process that anybody could learn in about half an hour. At first it was just another talent, something I could do that the rest of the crowd couldn't do.

I think Dorothy was the first one I began to practise with. Everything worked very well. I got more books, and read everything I could get my hand on about hypnosis and psychology. Before long, I knew as much about it as anybody could.

At first, I did things like stretching her out between two chairs, with her neck on one chair and her ankles on the other, and then I would stand on her. Later on, I got into age-regression—that was what really fascinated me—and then later, I got her into a somnambulistic trance and experimented with hallucinations and post-hypnotic suggestion. She was one of my best subjects and I really wanted to know everything there was to know about hypnosis.

When people found out I could hypnotize, I started doing a little bit of therapy. I used to help people who wanted to stop smoking, or who had headaches, or wanted to remember something they had forgotten. This was from the time I was eighteen to about twenty-three.

When I was living in St. Thomas, there was a boy there who was a pathological liar. His parents had taken him to all kinds of doctors and finally they asked me to come in. So I put him into a trance and went through an age-regression thing with him. He was adopted, and these problems he had were back before his adopted parents knew him.

When he got back to about six years old, he didn't want to come back. Everytime I asked him how old he was, he insisted on staying at six. Finally I got him to seven and brought him back a year at a time. Well his parents were just sitting there bug-eyed. After I got him out of it, they got all upset and called a doctor to find out if I had done anything to him.

The doctor came and talked to the parents and talked to the boy, and then we had a talk for about two hours. After we finished, he called the parents in and said he didn't think it was a good idea for them to bring me into their situation, and that as far as the process of hypnosis went, I knew as much about it as he had learned in medical school.

Soon after that, word got around to the Mormon church I was going to that I was doing hypnosis, and some of the people refused to come into the church if I was there, unless I repented. So I left.

First of all, people don't believe you can do it. It always starts as a joke. One night I was being made fun of about it at a party at Dorothy's sister's place. This one woman bet me five dollars I couldn't hypnotize her.

I walked over to where she was sitting on a couch. I put my thumb on her forehead and said, "You are stuck to this couch; you can't move." She was really trying, and the muscles stood out on her neck and arms, but she couldn't budge. Finally I told her she could relax and get up. Well, there wasn't a person in that room that wanted to have anything to do with me. They thought I was some evil kind of person.

I had some bad experiences with auto-suggestion. I played around with it, particularly in times of stress. I would auto-suggest happy or beautiful thoughts to myself, or get into sexual fantasies, but not be able to pull out of it. I'd fall asleep and then wake up in the middle of the night, unable to move. You can really feel panic in that space.

People began to think I had some weird kind of control over the women that were with me—control outside of the normal. It happened with Dorothy, and her family thought I had her as some kind of unwilling victim, but I never used it like that.

There is just so much misunderstanding about hypnosis that there was just no way I could do it. I'd love to get back into it, but to find a good subject without getting into all kinds of hassles is really difficult.

When LaSalle Park opened in the spring, Duke opened a candy-floss stand. He worked until the end of the season, and in the fall landed a job with the Morgan dance studios high-pressuring lonely women into paying twelve dollars an hour for dance lessons. But with the coming of spring, Duke itched to get back on the road.

When Duke spotted a want-ad for a job with the Barnard and Barry shows—at that time the largest travelling carnival in Canada—his problems were solved. He could travel, and be paid for it. He got on with the show as a "forty-miler," a carny expression for people who joined the carnival at one town, travelled to the next and quit. But Duke had other ideas; he wanted to be part of the show.

The carnival gave me a chance to travel, and it was also a community. Carnies do form a community and they do stick together, and it was the first time in my life that I felt I belonged to a community of people. I was very proud of the fact my father had been in the business so long and was very well-known. Ride owners, agents, and concession owners knew my father as a straight-shooter, a good operator, and a guy who never caused any hassle.

I was able to move around the carnival, not as a kid from the outside, but as the son of a carny, and people took it for granted I was a carny. I enjoyed the life. It was a travelling, nomadic kind of life. There was constant activity, the constant flow of new faces, and there was a sense of being on the inside and everyone else was outside—people we called marks.

When I first started on the show, I was an agent on the cork game joint, a hanky pank. You know, you shoot at packages of cigarettes with a cork gun. I had this tack I'd stick in the cork when I was showing how it was done—then I could take the tack out before the mark started shooting. Anyway, when a show is

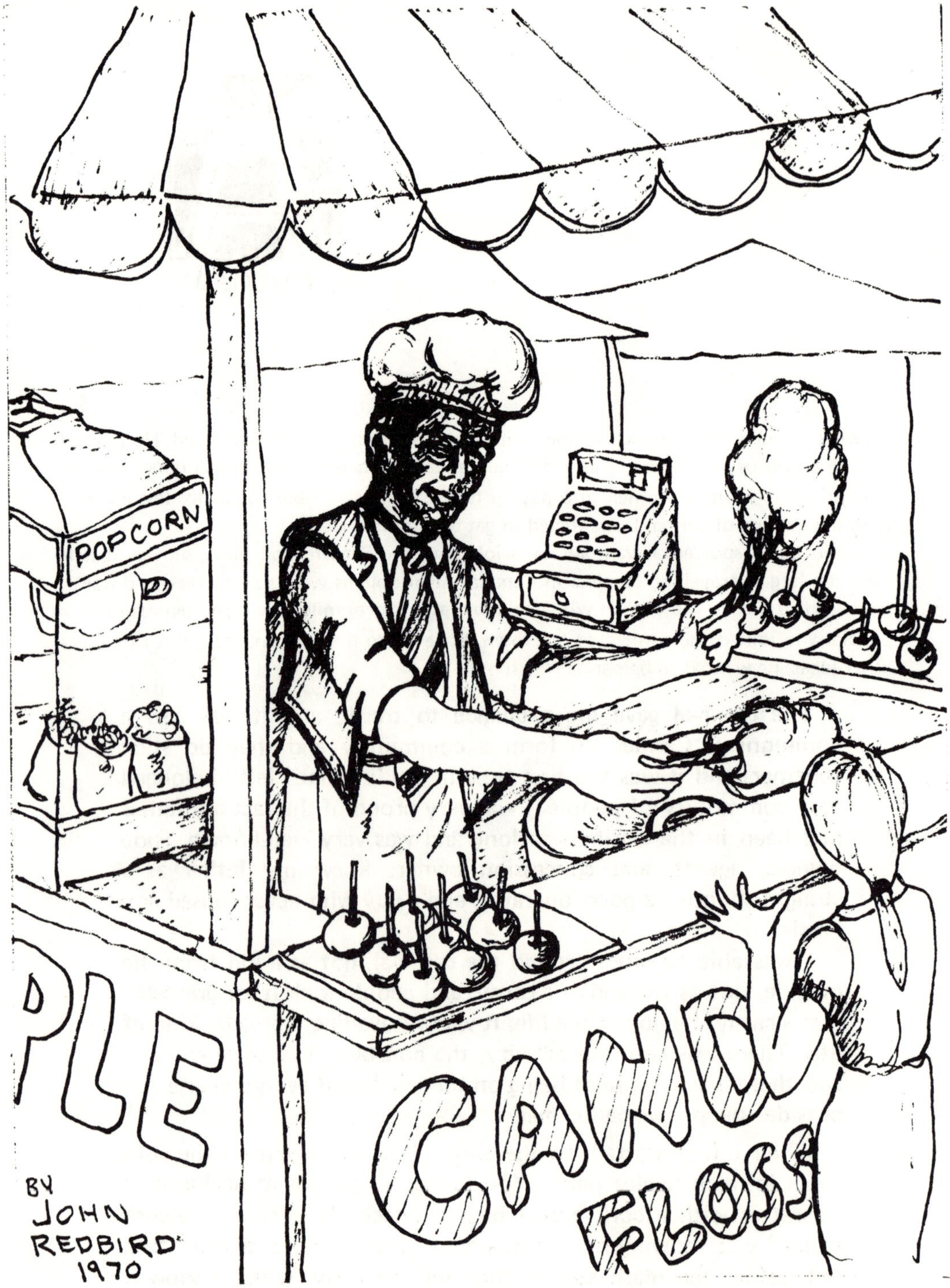
POPCORN
PLE
CAND
FLOSS
BY
JOHN
REDBIRD
1970

ready to move we have this thing we call a tear-down. Everybody would pitch in and help pack everything away for the move.

There was this French-Canadian guy who was a talker on the bally stage for the freak show. He was new and so was I. The people on the freak show were from the States and they didn't know my father, so I was just a forty-miler as far as they were concerned. And they started making disparaging remarks.

This guy Shoemaker, with no hands and no legs, he was saying things like, "There's going to be one dead Frenchman and one dead Indian around here in the morning." Because tear-down was really hard work. Well I decided I was going to show them. Come tear-down, I'm there and I'm working like hell. I discovered I had this knack for figuring out how things were put together so I could tell how to take it apart without doing the work twice. By the time tear-down was over, I was practically running the tear-down. The French Canadian had a really tough time.

The next day, we were at our new lot and everybody was standing around and I said, "I saw a dead Frenchman this morning, but I don't see any dead Indians." Everybody laughed, but they got the point. After that they started calling me Chief.

Duke was working for a bad tempered operator and finally blew up at him and quit—something you can't do in a carnival and expect to get another job—but Duke got away with it. Dorothy had a job as a bally girl on the freak show. She was tied to a cross on the stage outside the show and stood there while the barker gathered his crowd. At the end of the spiel she broke away from her "bonds" and led the crowd into the show.

Duke's new carnival family was slow to accept him. They certainly wouldn't play poker with a forty-miler. There was the Crocodile Woman; the seven-hundred pound Baby, Flo Johnson; Manuelita, the upside-down boy with no bones in his legs, who walked on his hands; the legless armless man who dealt cards and hammered nails; the two-faced man; Freddy the Frog Boy, with flippers for arms; and Doc, the Magician.

Doc had been a real doctor until he found his wife with another man and shot her. He served ten years, which he spent learning to be a sleight-of-hand magician. When he got out, he joined the carnival. Something of a philosopher, he and Duke became friends and Doc turned him on to a gaff—an act in the freak show. Duke became:

King of Torture

CHIEF KALI KHAN

Chief Kali Khan appeared on the bally stage with safety pins fastened through his nose, lips and cheeks. On the inside, he sewed medals and jewelry to his chest. The pins were a gaff—the centre was cut from the pin and the point soldered to the fastener. They were worn like earrings, but sewing the jewelry was for real. He thrust the needles through his skin and sewed jewelry and medals to his chest. The only real danger was from infection from the dyes used in the thread.

But now he was an attraction and part of the show. Now he could play cards with the rest of the freaks. He was accepted. He was part of their little community.

> As far as these people were concerned, I was a nobody. I was going to take tickets at the door or something. They certainly didn't want to have anything to do with me on a professional level. I did this trip as Chief Kali Khan to get around the performers a little bit.
>
> I found out that freaks were people, not just distorted human beings. They consider themselves performers and just a cut above the ride help. Of course, they have a closed community because they can't go out and wander around with the general public; it's difficult for them even to get along with carnies because of the way they look and the kind of life they have to lead, but when I joined up with the freak show, I became part of the community.

Duke so impressed one operator, an American, that he was offered a straw-boss job with a big American outfit, but Duke decided to stay with the Bernard and Barry outfit, which wanted to hire him as a sign painter—an artist.

The owners of the show, Willy and Jerry Bonner, were comic-style Chicago gangsters, complete with diamond rings, dark suits, big Cadillacs, and money to burn. The show, a thirty-six car train that travelled the carnival circuit out of Chicago every year, was a million-dollar business.

One ride took in between five and six thousand dollars a week, and they had thirty rides and up to eighty concessions. The show was a cover for underworld operations in loan-sharking, gambling, prostitution, and the numbers rackets, and Duke was their pet artist They liked to have him around. He had class.

> Willie and Jerry used to hang out at this particular restaurant in Welland. I go in and walk over to their table. I don't know if they were carrying guns or not, but they looked like they should be. They were really high-class criminals—even the way they talked, like Humphrey Bogart or George Raft. Everything was quiet and sort of whispered, like they couldn't have any kind of conversation without making it sound like a deal. And I walk in and Willie says:
>
> "Oh, hiya kid, how're ya doin'? Ya still paintin'? Ya ready to go on the road with us this year?"
>
> "Sure Willie, whatever you say."
>
> "I guess you've had a rough winter, eh?"
>
> "Yeah, well, I don't have much money."
>
> "Well, listen kid. How's forty bucks?" And he handed me a couple of twenties.
>
> "You're with us kid." And he'd introduce me to the shady characters sitting in the booth.
>
> "This is Duke. He's our show artist. He does all our painting. You should see the great work he does." And he'd go into this great long thing about my art, and how great an artist I was and they should respect me, and like that.

The carnival life solved Duke's financial problems, but it began to create marital strain. Dorothy was young and beautiful and everybody on the lot was attracted to her. Duke was jealous.

> **I couldn't allow her to walk across the street herself. I wanted her with me all the time, but at nineteen she was a woman, and I didn't have the assurance or the ability to cope with a woman. So I spent a lot of time trying to put her down. I won all the arguments, but I lost everything else. She just didn't want to be a mother to a twenty-year-old idiot who was going off in all directions without knowing who he was.**

Finally Dorothy left. She simply walked out of the house one night as if she was going to the store, and took off to Vancouver with another man. Duke was stunned and enraged, but there wasn't much he could do about it.

He spent the rest of the summer in Burlington Beach and headed back to Fort Erie in the fall. Dorothy came back but within a few weeks she was disappearing for days and nights at a time. Then she told Duke she was in love with a man named Bob St. Denis, and she left. Duke bought a twenty-two rifle and went looking for them. He was relieved when he couldn't find them.

When she left that time, I made up my mind right there: that was the end of my loving a woman. For the next five or six years I used women in every kind of selfish manner that I could. I hated women. I would play all these games to get women to fall in love with me, just so I could tell them to go to hell. I would get a great deal of joy out of causing pain and hurt to women.

Duke moved to Buffalo, and through Dorothy's brother, Bob Green, got a job operating a spring-making machine. He had no idea how to operate the machine, but Bob set up his own machine and then set up Duke's. It was four months before the management caught on, and Duke was laid off. Shortly afterwards, he decided to go to work for the Buffalo Creek Railway.

When I was working at the spring plant, there were three Canadians working there—Bob and myself, who were Indians, and this third guy. A guy downstairs got fired and he thought it was because these Canadians were hired, so he reported it to the border people. When the border patrol came around, the boss told the other guy to get lost. The patrol talked to us and asked us if we had work permits. We said no, but we told him we were Indians and they apologized for bothering us and went on their way. After I got laid off, I even received unemployment insurance from the States while I was living in Fort Erie. Indians can buy a car or anything else in the States and get it across without duty, as long as they maintain ownership. It used to work, but now with the draft dodgers and things, I don't know if it's still that way. I haven't crossed for years.

To qualify for the job as Yard and Interchange clerk, Duke had to compete in an I.Q. test with other applicants. Although he showed up half an hour late for the test and was told he wouldn't have time to complete it, he decided to give it a try. He was the first one finished, and a week later got a letter saying he was hired.

When he got to the job, a brakeman who had tried the test at the same time as Duke, and who had been trying for the job for years, showed him how to do it. The job was to keep track of all the boxcars coming in and to assign them to tracks where they would be hooked up for their destination. Duke had his own office and telephone, and a little red lantern.

I'm working there for a couple of weeks and I get a letter in the mail saying that last Tuesday I sent a car loaded with perishables for Minneapolis, to Kansas City. I thought this was funny, but the railroad took a dim view of it because it cost them about three thousand dollars to bring it back: but I was new on the job,

It's a long distance
In my past
And the memories
Are fading fast
Of that night we lay
Side by side
And looked across the bay
From our secret perch
High above the waves below.
We were not lovers yet,
Not in the true sense,
But in the truest sense we were.
We laughed a lot
And after we watched
Moonbeams rain down
Upon the ripples of the waves blown.
We caressed one another
With our eyes
And I loved you
More than words can tell.

and they could understand it. Well, another week went by and I get another letter saying I sent a car bound for New England to California—so I got fired.

The thing that impressed me about my short career with the railroad was that the guy that should have had my job—the brakeman—couldn't have it because he couldn't do the I.Q. test. That I should get that job—when I really couldn't do it at all—seemed to me real incompetence on the part of the railroad. Still, it was a little lesson I learned about the white man's way of testing.

Duke's next, and last, job was with a decal company in Buffalo. Within three months, he had picked up enough information and skill to work in any part of the plant's operation. His superiors were elated and offered to send him to the Kodak School of Photography for training. They told him he had a future with them.

Then one day I had lunch with a guy named Casey. He was sixty-five and had been with the company most of his life and was ready to be retired. He told me how good the company had been to him, how he had sent his kids to university, and had a house and a car and all that, but he told me, if he was my age, he wouldn't do it again. He'd go out on his own, because when you work for a company, you just end up retired. I finished my lunch, got my coat, and walked out. I never went back.

Duke had discovered the world of the working-man simply wasn't for him. But neither were the carnivals where, despite the excitement and constant change, he was haunted by a sense of emptiness and meaninglessness. He wasn't doing anything.

WHAT AN INDIAN WANTS TO DO, IS TO USE HIS HANDS, HIS BODY, AND HIS BRAINS IN A SPIRITUAL, CREATIVE, INTUITIVE WAY, AND MAKE A CONTRIBUTION AT THAT LEVEL. HE DOESN'T WANT TO BECOME AN EXTENSION OF A MACHINE.

So far, Duke hadn't really connected his difficulty in finding a meaningful way of life to his being Indian. Except for a defensive pride, his Indian orientation was very negative.

Finding my father and finding Dorothy and my Indian background certainly identified me. I was OK: but what I was identified with wasn't OK. That was another thing that bothered me. It would have been so much easier if my old man had been somebody—the prince and the pauper kind of thing that really intrigued me when I was a kid.

I thought, well someday, even though I'm a frog, I'll be discovered and then I'll be a prince. I had dreams about being discovered by my father or my brother or, in another sense, by the Indians: only to find out that every time I was discovered, it wasn't what I wanted.

If the Indian had been a great and noble spirit who had been beaten down, and the spirit was still there, it would have been OK: but as it was, they were beaten down and their spirit wasn't there. They weren't very good people to be identified with. To identify with them was to go backward. I was trying to find ways to prove that Indians really were the romantic notions I had about them.

But how can you take a philosophy or a way of life that is beautiful and cast it in the faces of the unbelievers, when all they do is laugh at you? It was nothing solid, or real, or tangible, that I could put my hands on.

The need to be recognized, to find a role, became a compulsion. Although Duke couldn't find anything real in the world around him, he found his fantasy made an impact on people. He began wearing costumes. He read that Frank Sinatra wore suits made only of mohair. He had a very expensive black suit made from it, and a black turtle neck sweater. A cane completed the costume.

After I left the railroad, I was going out with a girl named Marilyn. She was a very beautiful girl, from the upper-middle-class section of Tonawanda, just outside of Buffalo. We were very much in love, but she had all the upper-middle-class ideas about what I should have—success-orientation and all of that. Of course I didn't have any of these things happening for myself. It was very frustrating.

Anyway, I used to walk out to see her—it was about six miles. I would be wearing my uniform, complete with black overcoat and black hat. On my way, I would stop into a restaurant for a cup of coffee and I would play these games. I would sit there and start to raise the coffee cup to my lips and begin to cross my legs, then I would just freeze. For three or four minutes I would just sit there absolutely still, just long enough to bug the waitress and the people that were around. It was an action that was no action and people just couldn't cope with it at all.

What are you going to do with a guy who doesn't do anything? The waitress might say, "Are you all right?" and I would immediately move and say "Yes, I'm fine" and then freeze in the new position. It was a fun kind of thing.

It bugged the shit out of me that people were so conformist that they had a pattern for everything, including drinking coffee in a restaurant, and anything out of the norm was enough to freak people. I suppose too, it had something to do with being recognized. I wasn't being recognized by anybody, and the idea of living my life out in anonymity bugged me. I didn't like to be unknown,

The period between twenty and thirty was really difficult for me because I had no significant achievements of my own. I wanted to be somebody and have something done so that everyone who was putting down my dreams and my theories and my wild imaginings, would have to recognize me.

so I did a lot of things in those days so that I wasn't an unknown.

I wanted to communicate something to people. In this case, I wanted people to think that I was some kind of sinister, mysterious, and perhaps even evil kind of person: if that's what they wanted to think.

Really, I guess I wanted to keep who I really was a secret anyway, from everybody. That's a continuing sort of thing. The real me stays hidden behind any costume or role that I want to play at any given time. And I found it worked.

That period in Buffalo and Fort Erie was sort of a schizoid period. I would change daily, from my Indian costume with beadwork, Thunderbird disks and slit jeans, to my mysterious costume.

The closest thing to a permanent friend Duke had during this period, was his dog, Kim. A friend of his, Gordy, was the son of a kennel owner who raised German shepherds. Kim was the runt of the litter and was given to Gordy. Two years later, Gordy was killed when a tractor rolled over on him and Duke was the only person that Kim would relate to. They became inseparable in the old story-book sense.

Kim was really good for me. I never got hassled as long as I was with her. I wandered all over the down sections of Buffalo, New York, Toronto and Montreal. A couple of times she actually got me out of trouble.

I was at Crystal Beach one time, and about a dozen guys came wheeling into the park. They were an obnoxious gang and they were fooling around and pushing people. They saw Kim, who was under the bench I was sitting on, and the leader of this gang rushes up to Kim and growls at her. Well, Christ, she came out there like a bolt of lightning. She hit him about chest high and flattened him, and started tearing at his clothes. I jumped up and grabbed her, and that guy just crawled on his hands and knees as fast as he could go. Kim was really vicious when she got mad, and she could really be a mean-looking dog.

Kim's aggressiveness got Duke into more than a little trouble. A neighbourhood dachshund had been barking at Kim for weeks, and only Duke's watchfulness prevented retaliation. One day, Duke wasn't watching, and when the dachshund started its yapping, Kim attacked and killed the dog just like that.

Well, the dog's owner went out of her tree, and the first thing you know I've got the police on my back. They wanted to take Kim and destroy her. I said, "Look. I'll leave town right away and take Kim with me." They agreed if I got out of town in one hour they'd let it go. So I left for Hamilton.

Duke was strolling along a beach near Hamilton, in his black suit uniform and cane, when a girl, her curiosity obviously piqued by the outfit, introduced herself. The girl, Bonnie, took him home and introduced him to Barrie and Helen Lord, and to Lorrie Nixon, the operator of a coffee-house in Ottawa called the Womb. Lorrie and Helen took him to Hamilton's only coffee-house at the time, the Black Swan. Here he discovered still another breed of people—the beats.

I ran into a lot of other people who had similar sorts of ideas and similar sorts of frustration to mine, but they had found a way to create a little community for themselves. They could mind-fuck everybody else collectively. Everybody would sit around the Swan and talk about how they freaked out the straights. It was no different from what I was doing, but I was doing it alone. The reason they wanted to freak everybody was that they were looking for recognition, but they couldn't find it in regular channels, so they tried other ways.

We were all sort of in the same bag. We were creative, and had ideas and talents that were different from the norm. They were doing the same thing I was doing—which was nothing—but where else could you do nothing and have a group of people accept that that was the proper way to do things?

Duke was living with Bonnie, but the lack of money was a persistent problem. He noticed that none of the candy stores in Hamilton had candy-apples. Since job hunting had become a thing of the past, Duke borrowed some money, rented a house, and turned it into a kind of commune. The Black Swan drop-outs soon found themselves in the candy-apple business. Business boomed until the Christmas candy season glutted the market.

Duke dug out his paint box and went looking for work. He wandered around town until he saw a sign that needed repainting, then he went and sold the idea to the owner. He soon had a small paint shop open, with living quarters above. The place not only kept him alive but served as a gathering-place for his friends from the Black Swan. His association with the neophyte subculture soon attracted more attention than he was looking for—from the police.

The police used to come by just about every night. They'd knock on the door and they'd try it, and it would never be locked. They knew it was always open. Well for some reason, this one night they tried to come in without knocking.

Now Kim always sleeps at the foot of my bed or in the doorway. Anyway Kim bounds out of the room and leaps right over the stair-railing. I hear this horrible scream on the stairs. I go running out and there's Kim on top of a cop at the bottom of the stairs. He's trying to get his gun out, but he can't quite make it. I hauled her off him and he was just shaking. He started raising shit about vicious dogs, but I told him she was just protecting me, and he had no business sneaking in like that anyway. I never heard any more about it.

With the coming of spring, Duke decided to go back on the shows. He joined World's Finest Shows as a sign painter. Here, he found himself bunked in with an entirely different breed of cat—a female impersonator, one of several that worked the "girlie" show. Duke had little trouble coping with his new friends, once he got used to treating them like the women they wanted to be, but some of the "girls" really were girls. While he was painting a life-size illustration for the girlie show, the lead-stripper, Baby Doll—a French-Canadian girl named Gina—fell in love with him, and they decided to run off to Toronto together.

While they were packing the car, another carny, Blackie Reed, came running across the lot. He had just beaten up a mark and he thought the police were looking for him. The trio jumped into the car and took off. They hid out in a house on Spadina and searched the newspapers for news of the incident until they were sure the heat was off.

With his paint box, Duke got a series of odd jobs around Toronto, painting and re-painting signs, but he was keeping an eye out for a store. He and Blackie Reed, who was also part-Indian, were toying with the idea of opening a store selling Indian crafts. It was during this period that Duke changed his name for the last time.

I thought of many names—things like Yellow Claw, Big Bear, and Black Paw, but when the name, Redbird, came into my head, it was like a revelation. It didn't have any particular meaning for me at the time. That didn't come until later.

During a visit to his friends at the Black Swan, in Hamilton, another link in Duke's growing Indian identity was forged. Jim Neff, a tall ethereal man, with straight red hair past his shoulders and a beard that covered his chest, came over to Duke's table, pressed an object into his hand and walked away. Duke opened his hand and found a silver Thunderbird. Although he wore it constantly on a thong around his neck, he wasn't fully aware of its importance until years later.

Back in Toronto, Duke heard that Honest Ed Mirvish was renting out studios and stores on Markham Street for twenty dollars a month. A Mr. Simpson showed Duke through a row of vacant old homes, and when he heard Duke wanted to open an Indian craft store, he said he'd talk to Mr. Mirvish about it.

> Well I went into Honest Ed's store and through this hidden door kind of thing, and walked into the most sumptuous office I've ever seen. It had carpets this thick, a huge desk, statues of gold and silver all over the place, and all this rich drapery: and there was Mr. Mirvish, sitting behind this big desk in his big chair, and I'm standing there with dirty old blue jeans and a vest—no shirt. He wanted me to put up a teepee in an alley next to the store, but I thought a fort would be better. Anyway, I told him I didn't have any money, and he gave me seven hundred dollars and out I went.

Duke raced home with the money, after changing it all into small bills. He and Gina danced and laughed and yelled and threw the money into the air and stuffed it into garbage cans. They carefully retrieved it all and he and Blackie started work on the fort. Duke called it the Thunderbird.

While the fort was being put together, Gina was around less and less. For Duke it was a new kind of relationship with a woman, and a much less painful one.

> Gina was the funniest girl. I had decided I wasn't going to try and possess Gina—so we were good friends. Every few weeks or so she would tell me she had to get back on the stage. She would disappear for a couple of weeks, then back she'd come and tell me she had been dancing at the Victory Burlesque or someplace else. She finally left for good, but it wasn't for any particular reason. It was just that every time she came back I'd be connected to another girl. She accepted that, and finally just disappeared.

Back at the fort, Duke and Blackie—who had changed his name to Umtuk-built rough-bark, split-log palisades at the front and back of an alley, next to Honest Ed's. They added a long roofed hut along one side, a fourteen-foot teepee at one end and a totem-pole out front. With cartons of bark canoes, wooden tomahawks and quill boxes, ordered from the Department of Indian Affairs, they were in business.

It was shortly after the fort opened that I met Duke, and I began dropping into the fort several times a week. Duke and my sister, Marian, met during one of Gina's absences, and began an affair. A friend of Duke's from the Swan, Yvonne Van Hiddegum, moved into town and the trio worked in the fort. Duke set up an easel outside the teepee and

began doing Indian motif paintings on cowhide; these sold as fast as he could turn them out.

Duke and Yvonne split a flat in a house above a bootlegger's. The whole summer passed in a blur of parties, dancing, talking, and just plain freaking around the newly-born Yorkville Village; but as the tourist season fell off, so did business. Blackie was taking half of what money there was, Duke was taking the other half and when the season was over there was no money.

Toward the end of the season, Duke noticed two Indians with pot bellies and little grins on their faces, wandering around the fort. He got talking to them and they introduced themselves as Wilfred Pelletier of the Indian-Eskimo Association, and Isaac Beaulieu of the National Indian Council. They invited Duke to drop by their offices.

Duke and I had become good friends by the end of the summer, and it was obvious that he was going through some very heavy changes. It was around this time that the episode where he tore at his face, trying to rip out the Indian in him, took place. As business at the fort began to trickle away, Duke became more and more depressed and, in those days, that meant he started thinking about Dorothy.

I dropped in to see him one evening and found him painting a small portrait of a woman in red. He was transferring the red from his wrist to the canvas board. At first, I thought he was just using his wrist as a palette, but when he picked up a knife and cut a fresh gash in his wrist, I realized that he was painting the portrait in his own blood.

I don't believe in being alone. I don't know why. It's just my personality. I need to be loved. A lot of the time, I think that if people really knew me they'd love me, and then I think if they really knew me they wouldn't love me, you know?

Duke then connected with a strikingly beautiful, tall, brunette, sixteen-year-old named Kathy. She wanted to get out of town, and with business down to nil at the fort, there was little to hold Duke. They packed their bags and took off for Ottawa. Mr. Mirvish promptly took over the fort, put a roof on it, and set up for the Christmas rush.

Duke and Kathy looked up Lorrie Nixon in Ottawa, at the Womb—it had hair all around the entrance door—and found out the club was going out of business. Lorrie was dejected because he couldn't meet his rent and offered the club to Duke. Duke had sixty-five dollars in his pocket—the exact amount of the rent—and he was in the coffee-house business.

I was living in Ottawa and running the club, and this guy Basil Misca started hanging around. He was an architect, a sort of playboy type with a lot of money and a different pretty girl every time you saw him. He was trying to do the "in" kinds of things, but never quite making it. He was more interested in Kathy than he was in me, but he was taking this trip to Montreal one day, and I went with him.

In Montreal, we met a girl named Shirley Webb, and Basil offered her a ride back to Ottawa with us. We decided to go out to Ruby Foo's for dinner, and on the way out the conversation was mostly between Shirley and me. The same when we got to the restaurant. So we had roast duck, I remember, and when we came out, Shirley and I got into the back and continued our conversation, leaving Basil up front doing the driving. I think Basil was a little bugged by this because he started driving pretty fast, and we'd had a few drinks.

About half an hour from Ruby Foo's, the highway ended at this great cement barricade with a sign directing traffic onto a side-road. Well, we didn't make it.

Basil yelled, "Look out." I looked up and saw the barricade coming at us. I yelled, "Christ, I'm dead." and the world exploded.

The next thing I knew, I was in the front seat, half hanging out the front door. Shirley was screaming in the back, and Basil was slumped over the wheel. I couldn't catch my breath. I couldn't breathe, and when I finally did, the pain was something I had never experienced before. It was my back.

I looked into the back seat and there was blood all over everything. Shirley's face was unrecognizable. I crawled out of the car on my arms, then I tried to pull myself up on the door. I couldn't do it. I slid back down the door and tried to pull myself out onto the highway, but I couldn't do that either. I guess I passed out.

The next thing, I remember, was people. I rolled over on my back and somebody put a blanket over me. It seemed like an eternity, lying there on the highway. Finally they put us in an ambulance and headed back for Montreal.

After just getting out of an accident, then being wide-awake in an ambulance screaming down the highway at sixty or seventy miles an hour—that was another experience. By the time I got to the hospital, I was in a giddy mood and making all these wisecracks. They took x-rays, gave me some shots and wheeled me into the hall for the night. That night was terrible. The shots didn't put me out—they just numbed me so I couldn't do anything about the pain.

The next day, I found out I had fractured my third and fourth lumbar vertebrae. This was impossible. I had no money. I had to get back to the club. Everything was falling apart all over the place.

A week later, I figured it was time for me to go home. The doctor said if I could walk down the hall and sign myself out, I could go home. Great. So I threw back the covers, rolled out of bed and when my feet hit the floor it felt like somebody stabbed me in the back with a machete. He helped me back into bed.

They put a body cast on me and I was released a week later. I was supposed to take therapy and all that, but I couldn't afford it. I never did take any. It hasn't affected me much, other than I can't lift heavy weights.

Shirley had a fractured skull and she was in hospital for a long time. Basil had broken ribs, a broken hand and nose, and internal injuries. I ended up settling out of court for two thousand five hundred dollars. I paid off a lot of debts and did something I'd been wanting to do for a long time. I started a lawyer working on getting my named changed, legally, to Duke Redbird.

With Kathy as his waitress, turning everybody on, Duke was soon operating at a twenty-five cent cover-charge and the club was a going concern. He rented the room next door to the club and turned it into a studio, where he did Indian paintings and silk-screened Indian designs onto the leather bookmarks which he peddled to local stores.

Duke returned to Toronto just long enough to pick up my sister, Marian, my girlfriend, Janet, and me. We moved into the studio and went to work on the bookmarks. I still have callus marks from cutting that damn fringe. Duke designed a set of hasti-notes, with line-drawings in an Indian motif, and made a deal with a local printer to produce them. They sold as fast as they came off the press. People began to take notice.

Before we left Ottawa, Duke heard that a reporter from the Ottawa Journal was looking for him, to do a story. The idea seemed to electrify him. As an ex-reporter, the whole thing seemed routine to me, but Duke reacted with an intensity that I thought was all out of proportion to the interview's importance.

When the feature story came out, Duke glowed. As far as he was concerned, it was his first public recognition, and he was going to make the most of it. A few weeks later, Duke was asked to appear on a children's television program in Ottawa, and he was quick to take advantage of the fact that another door was opening.

We were all getting tired of the limited scene in Ottawa, and decided to return to Toronto. We packed everything we owned: art equipment, silk-screen equipment, suitcases, trunks, books, mattresses—the works, into a tiny Renault. Janet and I squeezed in on a mattress, between the load on the back seat and the roof. Marian, Duke and Kim crowded into the front seat and we trundled off to Toronto.

We developed a ritual for every service station we stopped at. Duke would pull up at the pumps and casually get out, Marian and Kim would get out the other side, then both would reach in and pull me head first out of the car, and then all of us would pull Janet out. The gas-jockeys just stood there with their mouths hanging open at all the humanity being hauled out of a car that looked packed after we were out of it.

When we got to Toronto, Duke discovered an old coach-house on Walmer Road that was almost perfect for a studio; almost, because it lacked toilets or running water. Those facilities were in the basement of a rooming-house in front of the coach-house; but we moved in, literally took snow-shovels to the dirt and sawdust on the floors, and set up the silk-screen studio.

Duke decided to drop over to the offices of the National Indian Council and the Indian-Eskimo Association. He re-introduced himself to Wilfred Pelletier and Isaac Beaulieu, and over a couple of beers, they talked about a mimeographed newspaper they had going—the Thunderbird.

WHAT REALLY TURNED THINGS ON FOR ME, WAS THAT ONE DAY WILFRED PELLETIER ASKED ME TO GO FOR A DRIVE WITH HIM. HE TOOK ME OUT TO THIS RESERVE. AS WE WERE DRIVING ALONG, HE WAS SAYING THINGS LIKE, "LOOK AT HOW THESE PEOPLE LIVE. THEY ARE OUR PEOPLE. ISN'T IT TERRIBLE THAT THEY HAVE TO LIVE LIKE THIS? DOESN'T IT MAKE YOU FEEL YOU WANT TO DO SOMETHING WORTH-WHILE AND WORK TO HELP THESE PEOPLE?"

THIS REALLY TOUCHED A CHORD IN ME.

HERE, FOR THE FIRST TIME, SOMEBODY WAS GIVING ME AN OPPORTUNITY TO DO SOMETHING FOR OTHER PEOPLE. UP TO THIS TIME, THE ONLY THINGS I HAD EVER DONE IN MY LIFE WERE FOR MYSELF. NEVER HAD I CONCENTRATED ANY EFFORT IN DOING SOMETHING FOR OTHER PEOPLE. THIS IS WHAT GOT ME SO EXCITED: THAT SOMEBODY WAS ASKING ME TO DO SOMETHING FOR PEOPLE

Duke ridiculed the amateur production and began rattling off all the things that a newspaper should have that this one didn't. They challenged him to do it better, and he accepted. Duke knew, of course, that I had been a journalist and had had several years of experience in putting out small publications.

Duke didn't have to do much talking to get me into the picture. We pooled our ideas, sat down at a typewriter and two weeks later the first issue of the re-vamped Thunderbird came out. It made an immediate impact.

As Duke became involved with the political organization of the NIC, he became more intense about the plight of the Canadian Indian.

LESS FORTUNATE THAN ME. I WAS THINKING THAT I WAS THE LEAST FORTUNATE, AND NOBODY HAD EVER CONSIDERED THAT I MIGHT HAVE SOMETHING TO GIVE TO SOMEBODY ELSE. SO THAT'S WHAT TURNED ME ON.

One of his Ottawa customers, Jack Cook, who was opening his Canadian craft store, asked Duke to go on a buying junket to reserves around Ontario. Duke was off on another leg of his education.

I had been to the Saugeen reserve to see my uncle—he's chief there now—and after I met Dorothy, I started going up to the Six Nations reserve at Brantford. I'd been to the Tuscarora reserve too, and to the Mohawks at Ohsweken. My first reaction was that I liked it. It was a free and easy kind of place without restrictions, and I dug that.

There weren't the social kinds of restrictions that you find in white society. There is nothing really expected of you; there are no social graces to worry about, and you don't have to conduct yourself in a particular kind of fashion. You can do your own thing and it's acceptable.

You go to bed when you get tired and you eat when you are hungry. Children are treated just like adults. It didn't seem to matter what age you were.

The poverty isn't as noticeable on the southern reserves as it is in the north and, at the time, it seemed like the best of all possible worlds. There was no high class or low class. Nobody bothers you about anything. I don't think much of reserves any more, but it took me a while to get behind what was happening on reserves.

Duke travelled through most of the reserves in Ontario, gathering material for Cook's store, the Four Corners. Apart from the success of the buying trip, Duke discovered that most reserve Indians were wary of him at first. He behaved too much like a white man to suit them.

They wondered whether I was an Indian or not. I had some idea in my mind of what an Indian was, and I was trying to play that role. I was faking it. People didn't know exactly what was wrong, but they knew something was. That doesn't happen anymore, because now when I go into a community, I am just myself, and myself is an Indian, but now I have all the background I didn't have at the time.

Duke began to explore Indian culture as it existed in Canada. He distrusted book-knowledge about Indians, especially if the books were written by white men. He talked to chiefs, medicine-men, old story-tellers, dancers, and just plain Indians.

While I was studying symbols in Indian culture, I found out a bird is always a messenger, and red, of course, is representative of the redman. So my chosen name meant that I was an Indian messenger of some sort. It wasn't until later, that I found out the Thunderbird is usually a red bird.

As editor of the Thunderbird newspaper, Duke had a medium for his message, but as he began to piece together his growing knowledge of the plight of Indians in Canada, he found himself coming to radically different conclusions from those of his friends at the NIC.

I noticed that there was a feeling of inferiority and insecurity—in fact a failure-complex—in both the NIC and the Indian-Eskimo Association. They were coming on with all these problems about how they didn't know how things worked. I was saying that they could do anything they wanted to. Finally I said, "Forget it, if you're going to think like that I don't want anything to do with you guys." After three issues of the Thunderbird, I left.

Coincidentally, so did I. Duke, his brother John and I had been working to get a craft store together on Avenue Road. Just before opening, Duke disappeared with a blonde bass-player who had been playing the second half of a female folk duet with Vikki Taylor in clubs around the Village. The landlord got uptight and threw new locks on the doors, but there was no budging Kim.

She hung around the store waiting for Duke, and wouldn't let anybody near the place. No matter how many times we dragged her away, she managed to get out and get back to the store. She was becoming quite sick. Finally the pound picked her up and destroyed her before Duke got back to town.

When Duke returned and learned what had happened, he was frantic and then severely depressed. I was very uptight. We parted wordlessly, and stayed parted for more than six years. Duke had his own path to travel.

He was attracting more and more attention in the mass media. He knew that controversy was the key to media attention, and he was quick to capitalize on any situation. When the controversy over the Canadian flag arose, while we still had the coach house, Duke thought Indians should have their say.

He designed a flag with a great black Thunderbird mounted in a yellow maple leaf on a red background. While my mother was sewing the prototype together, Duke was on the phone to the Toronto newspapers. Next day, Duke and his flag were front-page news.

The publicity worked. Duke began to receive invitations from socially prominent Canadian people, and he responded enthusiastically. Here, he thought, was his chance to tell influential people where it was at for Canadian Indians. They were charmed by his grace and wit, impressed by his intensity, and stimulated by his ideas: but nothing happened. It wasn't long before Duke had had more than his fill of liberal platitudes.

IT'S SO EASY FOR THE WHITE MAN TO COME ALONG AND BE GENEROUS WITH HIMSELF AND WITH ME, ABOUT THE THINGS HE'S GOT GOING FOR HIMSELF. THIS IS THE GREAT LIBERAL PATTERN. IF I FEEL THAT INDIANS ARE A DIFFERENT PEOPLE, THEN HE PUTS LABELS ON ME—LABELS THAT HE'S CREATED FOR HIS OWN PEACE OF MIND.

BECAUSE I FIND THAT THERE ARE UNIQUE THINGS ABOUT INDIANS AND THAT WE'RE A DIFFERENT KIND OF PEOPLE—DAMN IT, WE'RE DIFFERENT AND THAT'S THE WAY WE ARE, AND I'M NOT GOING TO BE CALLED A RACIST BECAUSE I HAPPEN TO BELIEVE THAT.

TO BE INDIAN IS TO BE UNIQUE, IS TO BE A PERSON WHO IS RELATED TO THE WORLD AND TO HIMSELF IN A SPECIAL WAY, A UNIQUE WAY, THAT IS INDIGENOUS TO THIS CONTINENT AND IS QUITE DIFFERENT FROM WHAT THE WESTERN EUROPEAN FEELS HIS RELATIONSHIP TO THE WORLD TO BE. INDIANS ARE MOTIVATED AT A

CREATIVE, PASSIVE, SPIRITUAL LEVEL—AS OPPOSED TO THE ACADEMIC, INTELLECTUAL APPROACH OF MOST WESTERN EUROPEANS.

Acutely aware that he was standing on a very shaky bridge between the world of Indian and white, Duke found himself developing revolutionary techniques to get his point across. The liberal reaction to his early stance radicalized his politcal posture.

> Most of the talks I was giving told people how much I hated the white man, yet I was going home with white friends and sleeping with white chicks. There was no question that a dichotomy was developing—but I really don't think it was dishonest. It was a political ploy. It's much like the story of a man who was selling a mule. He told the prospective buyer:
> "All you have to do is say, 'Giddyup,' and he'll go."
> Taking him at his word the buyer tried it. The mule didn't budge.
> "Not like that," the seller said, "like this." He picked up a large club, walked up to the mule and slammed him over the head with it.
> "Giddyup," he said quietly, and the mule moved out.
> "But I thought you said you just have to say 'Giddyup.'"
> "You do," the buyer smiled, "but first you have to get his attention."

Although Duke was hard on the white man, he was just as hard on the Indians. He jolted the Indian world with a concept that was directly opposed to many of their basic assumptions.

> **The thesis that Isaac Beaulieu of the National Indian Council and Wilfred Pelletier of the Indian Eskimo Association had, was that the Indian problem is economic—that all we have to do is solve the Indians' poverty problem and we have solved the Indian problem, period. It was an intuitive flash that told me that that was not the problem at all. The real problem was lack of cultural self-esteem.**
>
> **The key to the problem was to teach Indians that they could do anything they wanted to do: and to do that, you have to have cultural self-esteem.**

At first, the idea was laughed at, but when Duke put the idea into action, heads began to turn. He opened an Indian social club, cum coffee-house, cum discotheque, on Asquith Ave. It was the only place of its kind in the country, and it boomed. At its height, it had up to one thousand five hundred members, mostly Indians, and, of course, Duke was king.

Unlike most Indian social centers, which provided a broad range of welfare services and only the most conventional social rituals, like ping-pong and dances, the Thunderbird Club encouraged its members to be what they were, in any context they pleased. In line with Duke's idea of cultural self-esteem, once inside the Club, everything Indian was good.

Through his own experience and his relationships with club members, Duke became acutely aware of the peculiar problems of the urban Indian. Traditionally country dwellers, the thousands of young Indians flocking to Canada's cities found themselves caught up in a world they didn't understand, but Duke began to see a new kind of orientation to city life developing in these urban Indians. They were a new breed.

> The rate of Indian migration to Toronto has doubled in the last five years. As Western European society in North America becomes more compatible with the Indian life-style, Indians become more willing to get involved in that life-style.
>
> Forty years ago, we didn't have welfare programs; we didn't have manpower programs; we didn't have any of the socially oriented programs that we have today. If people didn't work, for work's sake, they died.
>
> But today we can accept the fact that there is a place like Yorkville Village with four or five hundred people who live there the year round, without working. Fifty years ago, somebody would have been down there throwing them in jail. The attitudes have changed and relaxed enough for Indian people to find the city more compatible with their way of life.

The new breed was creating new problems. A dichotomy of basic attitudes developed, between the urban Indian and the reserve Indian. Duke found it impossible to bridge the gap.

> I just got fed up with trying to convince Indians on reserves about anything. I came to the conclusion that there were a lot of lies going down. One of the biggest lies was that Indian reserves are the last bastion of Indian culture. The people who live on reserves are the last people in the world capable of being Indians in the real sense. An Indian who lives on a reserve simply can't exercise his traditional desires or his traditional way of life.
>
> It took me a long time to come to this conclusion. At one point I believed that the Indian reserves were sanctuaries for Indian culture and that's where the traditions were, and that's where you could best express yourself as an Indian person.
>
> The truth is, that the more I travelled on reserves, the more I found that it is the last place where Indian culture exists. It is the white society that has been encouraging this myth, and the Indians have picked up on the trip and believe it. It is a neat way to separate Indians from whites—the whites telling Indians that the only way they are going to stay Indian is to stay on the reserves: but the only way to be a real Indian, and express real Indian values is to get out into society, where things are happening.

When I was younger, I used to deliberately put down Indians in front of other Indians. I desperately wanted someone to tell me that the things I was saying—the things I had been told by whites—were wrong, but nobody seemed to be able to do it. So this is what I began doing with the club.

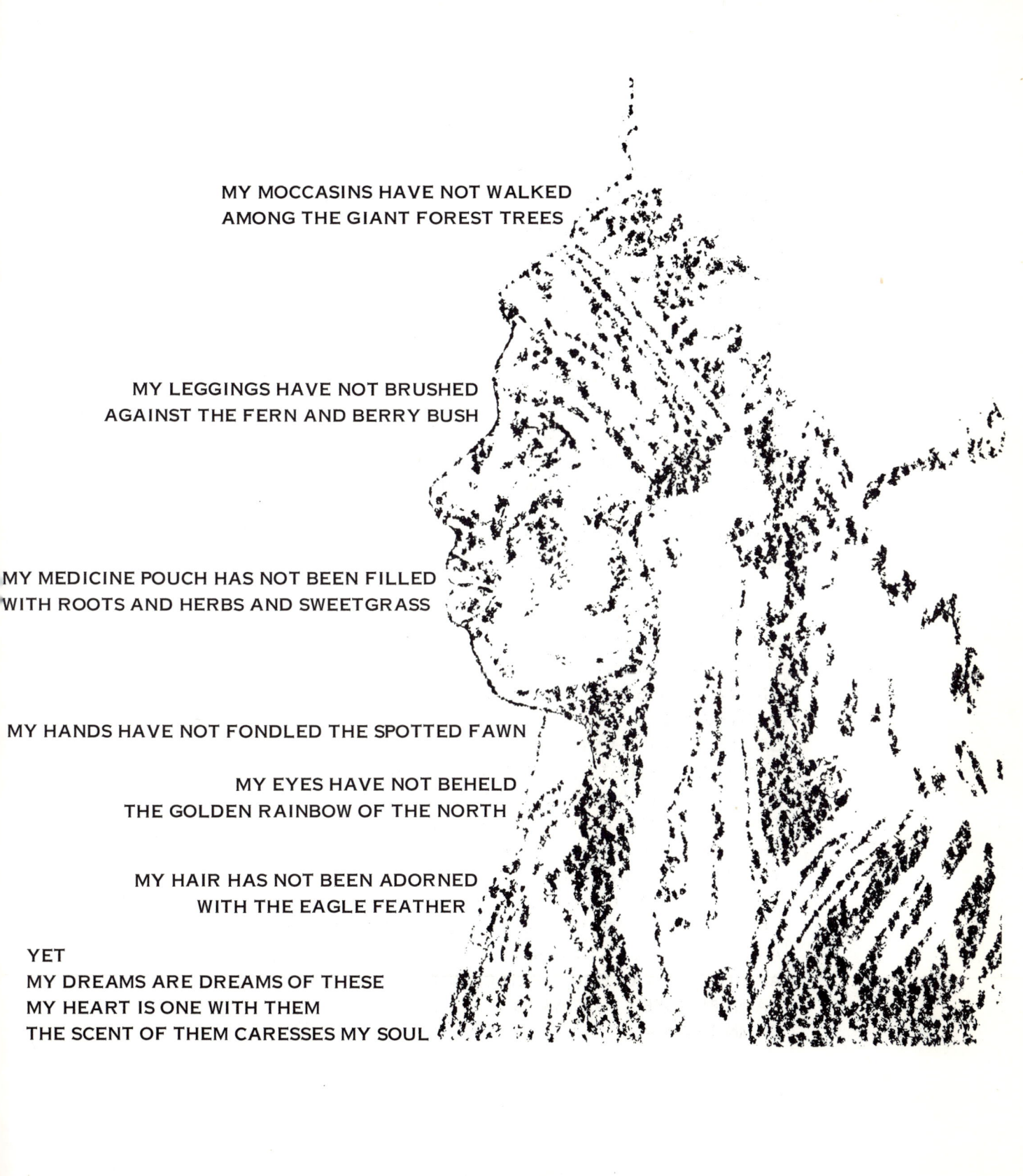

MY MOCCASINS HAVE NOT WALKED
AMONG THE GIANT FOREST TREES

MY LEGGINGS HAVE NOT BRUSHED
AGAINST THE FERN AND BERRY BUSH

MY MEDICINE POUCH HAS NOT BEEN FILLED
WITH ROOTS AND HERBS AND SWEETGRASS

MY HANDS HAVE NOT FONDLED THE SPOTTED FAWN

MY EYES HAVE NOT BEHELD
THE GOLDEN RAINBOW OF THE NORTH

MY HAIR HAS NOT BEEN ADORNED
WITH THE EAGLE FEATHER

YET
MY DREAMS ARE DREAMS OF THESE
MY HEART IS ONE WITH THEM
THE SCENT OF THEM CARESSES MY SOUL

THE FRAGMENTING SUNSET
OF A RED NATION
SPRAYED KALEIDOSCOPICALLY:
FACETS OF DIAMOND SOULS
ALONG THE WATERWAYS.
AND I SANG MY DEATH SONG,
FOR I WOULD NOT BEAR
TO SEE THIS PROUD NATION
SWALLOWED IN THE MOUTH OF PERFIDY.
SING, MY DRUM
IN A VOICE THAT'S LOUD
AND A VOICE THAT'S CLEAR.
FOR THE DRONING OF A THOUSAND JETS
AND THREE MILLION CARS
AND FIVE BILLION MACHINES
WILL DROWN YOUR TONGUE.

I CAN DO NOTHING.
LIKE THE BUFFALO I LIE,
MURDERED ON THIS CONCRETE PRAIRIE.
AND MY BONES BLEACH YELLOW
IN THE SMOG
OF ALL THOSE CHIMNEYS,
AND THE EXHAUST OF ALL THOSE CARS.
WHERE IS ONE SPRUCE OR PINE
THAT STILL REFLECTS NATURE'S GREEN?
THEY'RE ALL COVERED WITH THE
TINSEL OF TECHNOLOGY
AND THE STAR OF DAVID.
LINCOLN'S PENNIES NOW REPLACE THE GRASS
AND ROOSEVELT'S DIMES
ARE THE BY-WAY FOR BIRCH CANOES.
DAMN EUROPE'S BASTARDS.
DAMN THEM ALL.

As part of his cultural self-esteem program, Duke formed the Thunderbird Dance Troupe. The dancers made their own costumes and worked on traditional dances. They were an immediate success, both inside and outside the Club, but reaction to the Club wasn't all favourable. The fact that the Club stayed open all night and got a reputation for wild parties upset the more conventional members of the Indian community, but the young Indians loved it.

Duke, with a foot in both the white and the red worlds, was beginning to see how they were different and how they were the same. He had a ready audience in the bull-sessions at the Club.

> When I point out to Indian people that a concept like the guaranteed annual income is an old concept to the Indian people, they say, "Well, how is that?" I point out that nature provided a guaranteed annual income, and the white man has just now discovered that the best way to get along is to have a guaranteed annual income. He is merely discovering something that we knew all along. When you can make these kinds of comparisons, Indians go home feeling better about being Indians. That's the kind of thing I was looking for but couldn't find, when I was a kid.
>
> I am continually looking for more ways to explain what is happening in North America, because I believe Indians have already gone through all the processes. Anything that happens in North America has a connection compatible with Indian thinking.

Duke adopted the idea that man and his social organizations are influenced by their geophysical environment, and from this point of view, the differences between Indian and white became even more evident.

> *Indian people have picked up the geophysical vibrations of North America and manifested them in an intuitive, spiritual, passive way. Therefore, they have never been in danger of upsetting the ecology of North America. Indians, as a race, are a femininely oriented group of people and adapt themselves to their environment rather than change it to suit their short range needs.*
>
> **But the white man is basically a masculine individual—an aggressive, competitive, physical kind of personality. When he picks up those same North American vibrations, he manifests them in a chaotic way. He does not have the passive balance that is necessary. The only way this balance can come about is through a complete marriage of the two cultures, in such a way that we can produce a new North American personality that has both the yin and yang of the North American continent.**

No priest told her she was mine.
No ring bound her to me.
No ceremony has sanctified her soul.
No paper has seen her name,
Yet——
Loving hands sewed the beads on my moccasins.
Shining eyes greeted me after the hunt.
Tender caresses put my spirit to sleep.
Silent words told me I was brave.
For——
The Great Spirit had beheld her virtue.
His voice had led her to me.
Our Mother, Earth, received us both.
We became one with their blessing.

The Thunderbird Dancers were gaining country-wide fame. They got an invitation to tour the western provinces and fifteen of them took off on the junket.

While they were in Winnipeg, the NIC was holding its annual elections. According to a pre-arranged scheme, the dancers attended the meeting, nominated Duke for vice-president and voted him in, en bloc. The older, more conservative members were flabbergasted at the coup.

Back in Toronto, Duke had established a relationship with a beautiful Indian girl, an Ojibway, who had been coming to the Thunderbird club. They began living together.

> Elaine is one of the few people that I truly love. But part of the desire that was there, as well as being in love, was political; Elaine was an Indian, and really, I didn't feel strong enough to marry and have children by a white woman. My position in terms of the National Indian Council and what I believed as part of my little red-power trip, was so much involved with the Indian community that I felt I would have been a hypocrite to teach all those things about the white man and then turn around and marry a white woman.
>
> Elaine is so completely Indian that if you asked her what it was like to be an Indian she would just smile. It just is her space. The strangest thing about her is that she doesn't talk, but she is capable of communicating every nuance of her thought and feeling. She is a classic example of the Indian space.
>
> **I had always assumed that I wasn't the family type of man—that I would never be able to be a husband or a father. I just assumed that those spaces weren't in me. Elaine brought out that family-orientation to a fantastic degree. Of course when the kids came along, a boy, Jay and a girl, Nahanie, it was a tremendous event in my life.**
>
> **Up to the time Elaine got pregnant I thought I would never have any children. I thought that because Dorothy and I didn't have any children, it was my fault—that I wasn't capable of having children.**
>
> **Elaine is the only woman I would want for the mother of my children. I really have no desire to have more children by any other woman.**

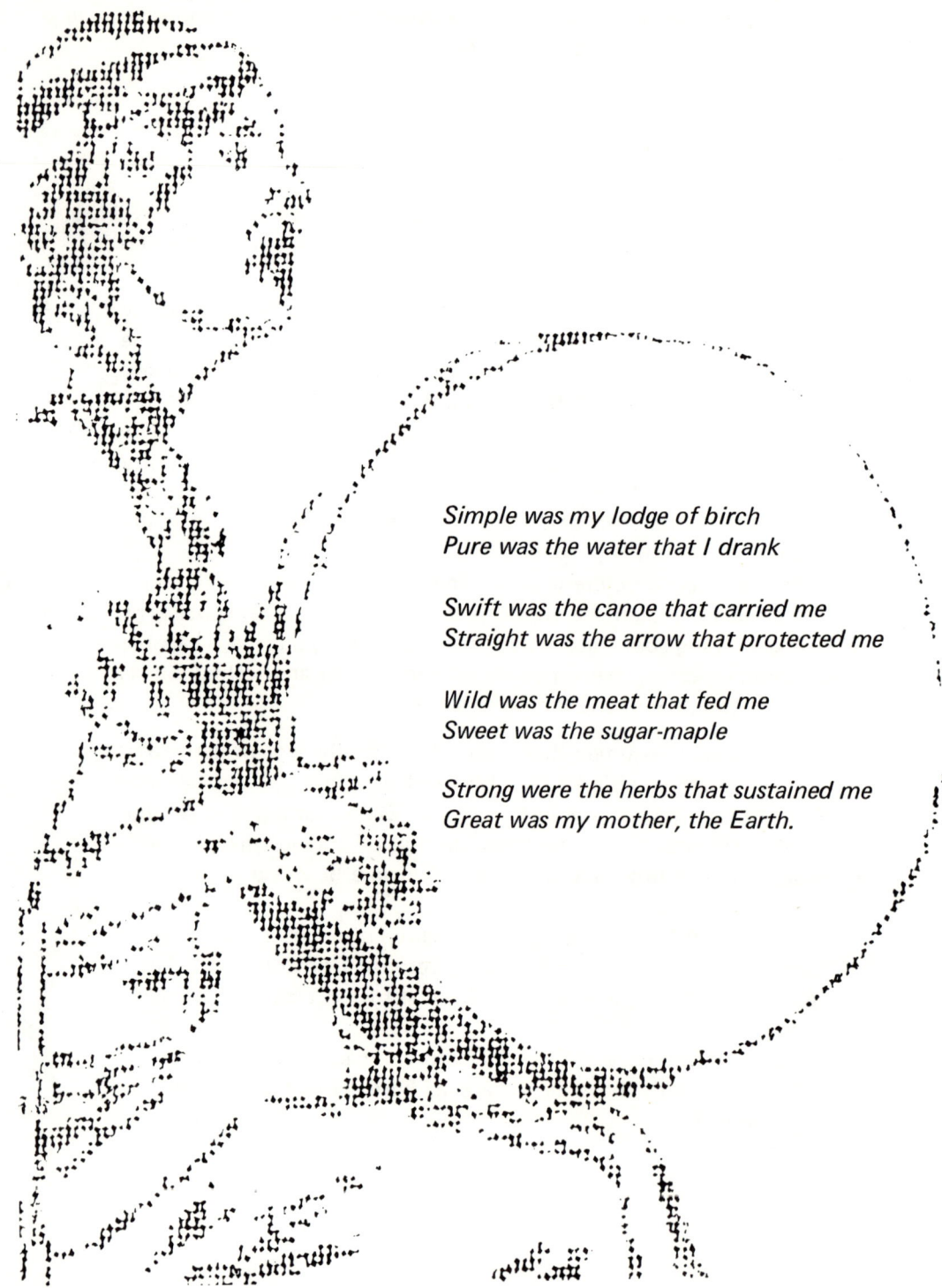

Simple was my lodge of birch
Pure was the water that I drank

Swift was the canoe that carried me
Straight was the arrow that protected me

Wild was the meat that fed me
Sweet was the sugar-maple

Strong were the herbs that sustained me
Great was my mother, the Earth.

Indian culture isn't disappearing in the cities—it's simply going through processes of change like anything else. The relationship Indians once had to their moccasins, they now have to their boots; the relationship we once had to our teepees, we now have to our apartments. The culture lives. It is always there.

There was a small group in the Thunderbird club who were all for stealing guns and taking off into the hills, à la Castro. Duke sidetracked them with the same techniques he had used with the Tyrants. They developed complicated plans for taking over whole sections of the country. Meanwhile, Duke was conducting his campaign to build up cultural self-esteem among the Indians.

Invitations to speak to church groups and social organizations poured in, and Duke launched a well-publicized attack on white society.

THE WHITE MAN IS A VICTIM OF THE WORLD HE CREATED FOR HIMSELF TO LIVE IN—OUT OF THAT COMES HIS BARBARIANISM. NOW HE'S A VICTIM OF THE POLLUTION AND WASTE HE CREATED. HE IS A VICTIM OF HIS OWN MENTAL POLLUTION. THE CREATION OF ETHICS, POLITICAL GAMES, PHILOSOPHIES, RELIGIONS, THE PATTERNS OF MORALITY AND ALL THE REST OF IT—HAVE UPSET HIS MENTAL ECOLOGY AND THIS MENTAL IMBALANCE IS THE PROBLEM.

THE WESTERN EUROPEAN MAN IS MORE TO BE PITIED THAN ANYTHING ELSE, BECAUSE HE IS IN A STATE OF INSANITY—NOT ABLE TO MAINTAIN A BALANCE BETWEEN THE VARIOUS FORCES OF HUMAN CAPACITY. THE PHYSICAL LEVEL IS THE ONLY LEVEL ON WHICH WESTERN EUROPEAN MAN HAS MADE ANY PROGRESS. ON OTHER LEVELS HE HAS BECOME A VICTIM OF HIS OWN MENTAL POLLUTION.

YOU'LL FIND A LOT OF GOOD PEOPLE IN WHITE SOCIETY WHO HAVE SORT OF CLEANED OUT THEIR OWN SEWERS. AT LEAST THEY HAVE FILTERED THE POLLUTION TO A POINT WHERE THEY CAN SEE A BETTER WAY OF LIVING, AND RELATING TO THE WORLD AROUND THEM, BUT ALL OF US ARE VICTIMS OF THE CONDITIONS PRODUCED BY POLLUTED INDIVIDUALS.

THE INDIAN HAS HAD FORTY THOUSAND YEARS IN NORTH AMERICA AND HE HAS LEARNED TO LIVE HERE. THIS IS A FUNDAMENTAL DIFFERENCE BETWEEN THE INDIAN AND THE WHITE CULTURES. THE WHITE THINKS HE MUST HAVE DOMINION OVER HIS ENVIRONMENT AND, AS A RESULT, IS GARBAGING HIMSELF RIGHT OUT OF EXISTENCE.

WE ARE GOING TO HAVE TO TEACH THE WHITE MAN THE INDIAN WAY OF LIFE. IF WE DON'T, HE IS GOING TO KILL US ALL.

The Indian has avoided much of this pollution by being protected from it. The Western European has, in his own peculiar way, saved the Indian from the kind of psychological pollution I'm talking about, by simply not allowing Indians to become involved in it. It's sort of an exclusive club.

Indians have always realized that there are distinct advantages to being outside

the system—through prejudice or whatever. So we do not create the same kind of difficulties that the United States is experiencing, with black people wanting to become facsimiles of white society and sharing their power structure. Indians have had little desire to do that, because it is not what they are about as a people. That's one of the reasons Indians never became slaves.

It became cheaper for the Spanish, English and French to go to Africa and collect native Africans, bring them over here in boats and train them to work in a North American environment—it was cheaper for them to do all that, than to try and get an Indian to work. The Indian, even today, doesn't want a job. He wants a meaningful role, and you can't buy him off with goodies.

THE WESTERN EUROPEAN MAN IS A MAN WHO EXTENDS HIMSELF PHYSICALLY, BUT INDIANS EXTEND THEIR SPIRITUAL SELVES, SO THE EXTENSION SPIRITUALLY, IN AN INDIAN COMMUNITY, IS AS GREAT AS THE EXTENSION PHYSICALLY, IN A WHITE COMMUNITY. THE INDIAN CULTURE IS A SPIRITUAL CULTURE—THAT OF THE WESTERN EUROPEAN IS A PHYSICAL CULTURE.

THE BLACKS REPRESENT THE EMOTIONAL NATURE OF MAN, BUT TO BE A COMPLETED MAN, YOU HAVE TO HAVE ALL OF THE FACULTIES TOGETHER, EXPRESSING THEMSELVES, AND THAT IS SLOWLY COMING ABOUT IN NORTH AMERICA. THIS PHYSICAL MAN WITHOUT A SOUL IS BEGINNING TO GROPE FOR A SOUL, AND HE WILL FIND A SOUL, I'M SURE, IN THAT INDIGENOUS AMERICAN MAN—THE INDIAN.

White men just don't think like Indians. Their reality just isn't the same. They are in a completely different world. They don't see a chair the way we see a chair—even though they are using the same kinds of brains and eyes. Perception among peoples can be really different, in terms of the relationships they have with the world around them.

Anyone who tries to create parallels between thinking in European and Indian America is just wasting his time. Western man wants to see parallels so he creates the damn parallels, but to an Indian, these parallels just don't make sense: because they don't exist outside of the white man's mind.

If a Western man wants to create parallels and write them down in books and give lectures about them to his own people, that's all right. It makes sense to him. It doesn't make sense to me, or any other Indian I've talked to. It's like a Martian coming along and deciding that cars are the rulers of the earth and humans are the parasites that live in them.

I'm not basing my thinking about white society on American imperialism alone; I'm basing it on British imperialism, French imperialism, and German imperialism. Any Western European country worth its salt, in its own eyes, has embarked on some kind of exploitation of other people.

The society we live in doesn't encourage humanity and generosity, and charity, and those kinds of things. When I watch television, I'm encouraged to drink such-and-such a brand of beer, or to drive such-and-such a brand of car. There are no commercials on television encouraging me to be a nice guy. Madison Avenue isn't trying to motivate people toward being more humane. They are only trying to motivate them to be bigger and better consumers.

You know, things are going to get better for the Indians, but not because the government chooses to be more humane. It is simply because the government is going to become more efficient. It is only in the name of efficiency and expediency that we are getting any kind of recognition or reform in this country; it is not out of love of humanity. Whites don't seem to be capable of those kinds of feelings.

There's something about the Thunderbird that I really connected to. I realize you still have to do your own trip in life and all that, but I did have this feeling about the Thunderbird as a symbol. I've always had Thunderbirds around me. It seemed to be a very lucky symbol. Everything I attached it to seemed to work.

It all started when I was in Buffalo. I bought these beaded Thunderbird disks that I wore on the slits in my jeans. I wore beaded Thunderbird necklaces, but I was forever losing them. Girls would take them. Every time I got connected to a chick, she'd want to wear the necklace and I'd end up losing it.

As Duke explored the realities of Indian culture, he became intrigued with the use of symbols and totems. He began to realize that these seemingly fanciful relationships to animals and birds were in fact, very far-reaching psychic realities. In his own life, the Thunderbird had played a tremendous role.

One night at the Thunderbird club, a young Indian came in drunk and began smashing the place up. Duke kept out of his way and let him work out his rage. When the man came into the kitchen where Duke was standing, Duke instinctively clutched the silver Thunderbird he had worn around his neck for four years. The man stopped in mid-stride and began apologizing profusely, and then left. When Duke woke up the next morning, the Thunderbird was gone.

I have this Thunderbird ring, and I never take it off. That's why I didn't worry about the Thunderbird when it disappeared. There were enough Thunderbirds around. I had the Thunderbird ring, the Thunderbird club and the Thunderbird flag; I drove a Thunderbird car, and there were the Thunderbird dancers.

I was getting into a space at one time, when I was depending too much on this symbol, and there was getting to be more to it than I wanted to be connected to in that way. The more I got connected to Thunderbirds, the harder it was to think rationally about what I was doing. I didn't want to have that kind of a relationship to a symbol. I don't like being dependent on those kinds of spaces, so I began to move away from it a little. I just made it a less important aspect of my life.

NEMKE BENISHE
BIRD OF THUNDER
BIRD OF SPIRIT
BIRD OF TRUTH AND EVERLIGHT.

IN A REMOTE AND SUB-CELESTIAL DAWN
EMBRYONIC FLUID CAULDRONICLY BUBBLING
PRIMAEVAL INSULAR CRYPTIC ABYSS
ABSENT EMPTY HOLLOW VACUUMED WOMB.
THE COSMIC EDEN.

INTELLIGENCE SLUMBERED, SHINING DROPS OF LIGHT
DREAMING IN COSMIC SLEEP, SOMNAMBULISTIC SLEEP
DEEP DEEP SLEEP, EVER DEEP THROUGHOUT THE COSMIC
                NIGHT.

NEMKE BENISHE
BIRD OF THUNDER
BIRD OF SPIRIT
BIRD OF TRUTH AND EVERLIGHT.

NEMKE BENISHE ROSE ON PSYCHIC WINGS
AN IMAGE FORMED AND THEN REFORMED
IN PSYCHIC EYES
IMAGE FIRST, THEN SIGHT
WHEN THE EYELID LIFTED THE IMAGE
FROZE PSYCHICALLY, MATERIALLY, FOREVER.
THIS THEN WAS CALLED CREATION.
NEMKE BENISHE
BIRD OF THUNDER
BIRD OF SPIRIT
BIRD OF TRUTH AND EVERLIGHT.

COSMIC EMANATIONS BLUEPRINTING, PROGRAMMING
COUNTLESS CORRIDORS OF NUCLEAR MAGNETIC
              PATTERNING
MOLECULAR CIRCUITRY.
WEAVING REFINING MOULDING DEFINING RENDERING
OTHER CONSCIOUSNESS; THE LANGUAGE SONG AND
              MYTH
NEMKE BENISHE
BIRD OF THUNDER
BIRD OF SPIRIT
BIRD OF TRUTH AND EVERLIGHT.

Duke was quick to see how symbols functioned in the world around him. The American eagle and its regal domination over the skies, was an obvious example, and the oriental tiger with its ferocious cunning and mystery was another. In that light, Canada's national symbols were really comical, particularly to Indians.

The fact that Canada has the beaver as its symbol is, to Indians, foolish. Beavers go around cutting down trees and upsetting the whole ecology of the woods. When everyone else has gone to bed, they are working away. The parents build the lodge, then when the kittens grow up, the parents move out to make another lodge and the kittens take over: and that's what's happening in Canadian society today.

The beaver cuts down a tree that took about seventy years to grow up, just so he can chew off the top leaves when he gets the tree down. Isn't that what Canadians have done to this country? They came along and sort of chopped it up to get the resources at the top. In the meantime, they have polluted the lakes and skys and upset the whole ecology.

See how the beaver works all night
Without light
In the darkness he builds his dam
With limb and branch, mud and sand.
From dusk to dawn
His toil goes on and on and on.

Then tomorrow, you will see,
A bubbling stream becomes a pond
And later on, a stagnant lake
And all the creepy, crawly creatures
Will crawl down
And make a home within that putrid pond
With snake, frog, snail, and crab
These are neighbors the beaver will have

But the deer, bear, lynx, and fox,
Raccoon, moose, wolf, and hawk
Will move far away
To find a place the beaver hasn't been
Where clear, cold, clean water
Still flows
Living, laughing, tumbling, liquid life
Waterfalls, brooks and streams
These are the highways of life's dreams.

My son, do not become a beaver,
And build for yourself a dam,
For this is what the white man does
With his brick and stone and sand,
'Til his mind is like that lake
Filled with weird, wicked wretches
That give no peace,

Then he cries to his creator in desperation
Please God, my God
Deliver me from dam-nation.

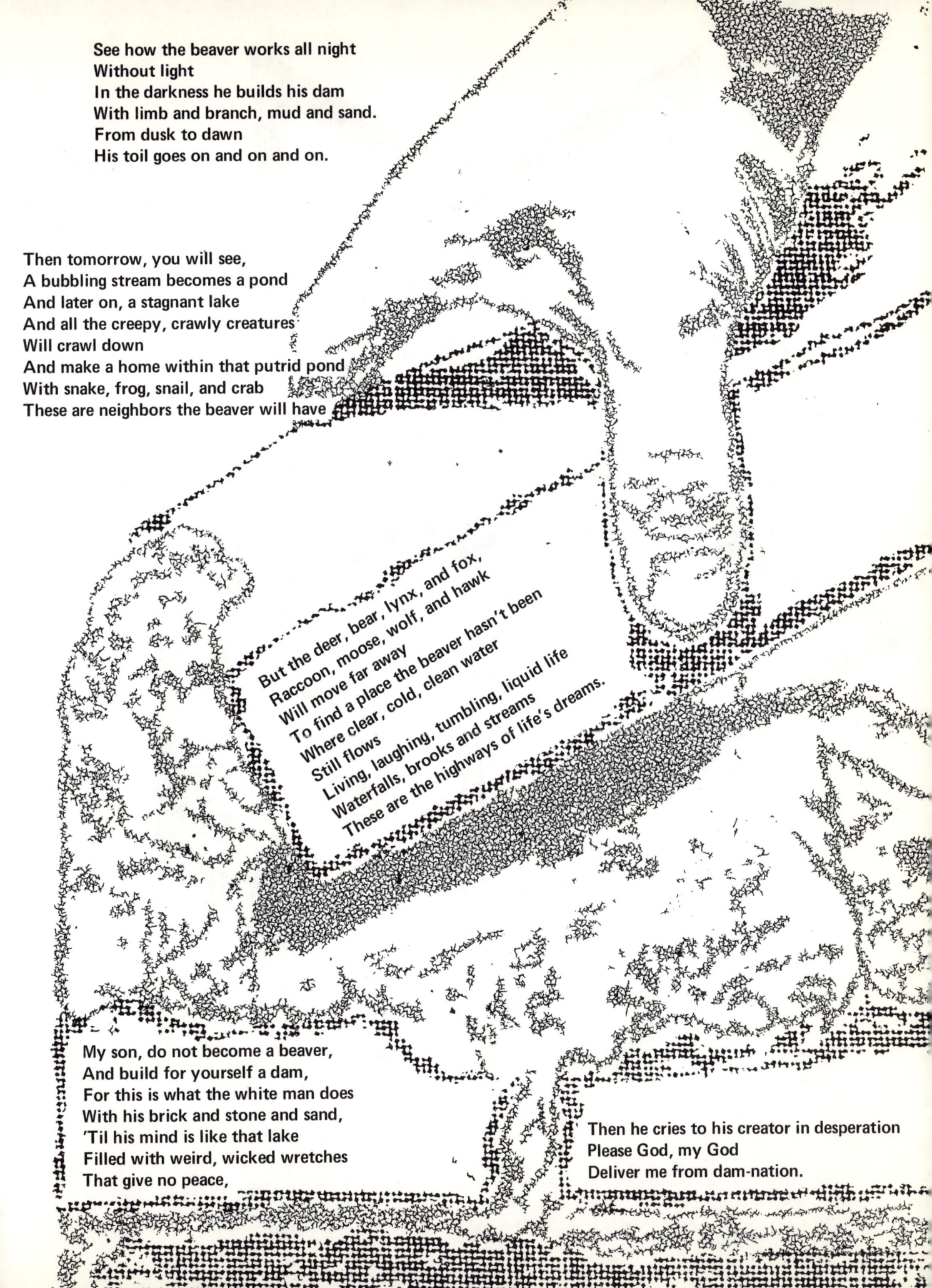

It was really interesting to see what symbol Canada used when it wanted people to buy Canadian—it chose the symbol of the moose. Well... to an Indian, the moose is the most ridiculous, stupid, idiotic, bungling animal in the whole forest. There is even a legend as to how the moose got that way.

It happened that Mother Earth was handing out clothing and so on, to all the animals. The animals gathered, and came up to choose the kind of outfit they wanted. The robin asked for a red breast and a brown coat; the raccoon got a little black mask and rings on its tail, and so on, but the moose was so stupid and dumb, he couldn't make up his mind about anything, and he just stood there throughout this whole process. Finally when everybody had what they wanted, there was nothing left except an old discarded buffalo-skin with the hump still on it, some antlers that nobody else wanted because they were so big and funny-looking, and these great clod-hoppers of feet, and so on. This was what the moose ended up with, and isn't that just representative of our economic policies—Canadians can never make up their minds about what they want. I must say, I find something appealing about the poor stupid moose.

Duke's activities with the NIC took him away from the Thunderbird Club more and more often, so his brother, John, took over effective management. The NIC, with Yves Theriault, then director of cultural programs for the Department of Indian Affairs, was developing the concept of the Indian Pavilion for Expo.

The Pavilion, for Duke, was a symbol of the modern Indian in Canada, and he began to work for Indian control over the project. He submitted a poem which became the theme for the pavilion.

All the money for the expo project had to come from the government and so the government had us hamstrung. The Centennial Commission refused to allow the National Indian Council to develop the Pavilion and they took it over themselves. They just didn't believe that we had the ability to pull it off. I thought we did.

Disillusionment was setting in within the NIC itself. Conflicts between treaty and non-treaty Indians complicated every issue. The non-treaty, and generally urban Indians were able to take over political control of most of the formal organizations, but the lack of dedication at the grass-roots level, and the growing resentment of the non-treaty faction's power structure by the treaty Indians, crippled the organization badly. The lack of confidence on the part of the Centennial Commission was the last straw.

Being vice-president of the National Indian Council was like being vice-president of nothing. The Thunderbird Club was more real, as an organization. I could see where it was going—nowhere—so I resigned at the end of my term. It folded a little while later.

I don't think the NIC, or the Indian-Eskimo Association are effective places for developing personal roles, simply because the day of that kind of organization is over. Pyramid organizations, as such, are obsolete. That's the reason I got out of most of the organizations I belonged to. I realized that Indians are too late with that kind of organization.

MAY YOUR FORM REFLECT
THE SYMMETRY OF OUR WIGWAMS AND OUR TEEPEES.
MAY YOUR STRUCTURE INCORPORATE
THE STRENGTH OF OUR LONG-HOUSES BOTH EAST AND
                                                                   WEST.
AND MAY YOUR WALLS CREATE
THE WARMTH OF OUR FIRES
THAT HAVE BURNED A HUNDRED THOUSAND YEARS.

MAY YOUR COLOURS EXPRESS
THE PAGEANTRY OF OUR CEREMONIES.
MAY YOUR TAPESTRIES WEAVE
THE STORY OF OUR GREAT MEN BOTH THEN AND NOW.
MAY YOUR FABRICS PORTRAY
THE CONTRASTS OF OUR CULTURE
THAT HAS LIVED A HUNDRED THOUSAND YEARS.

MAY YOUR FURNISHINGS TELL
THE SIMPLICITY OF OUR WANTS AND NEEDS.
MAY YOUR ACCOUTREMENTS SPELL
THE MULTIPLICITY OF OUR TONGUES BOTH OLD AND
                                                                   NEW.
MAY YOUR DESIGNS WHISPER
THE TALE OF OUR LEGENDS
THAT HAVE BEEN TOLD A HUNDRED THOUSAND YEARS.

MAY YOUR FIXTURES CAST
THE LIGHT OF OUR LEARNING.
MAY YOUR SHADOWS PROJECT
THE MYSTERY AND DEPTH OF OUR RELIGIONS BOTH
                                        REMEMBERED AND FORGOTTEN
MAY YOUR FOUNTAINS RECALL
THE BUBBLE OF OUR LAUGHTER AND THE SILENCE OF
                                                              OUR TEARS
THAT ECHO ACROSS A HUNDRED THOUSAND YEARS.

MAY YOUR FLOOR COMBINE
THE PAST AND FUTURE OF OUR PEOPLE,
MAY YOUR CARPETS SPIN
THE MOSAIC OF OUR COMPLEXITIES BOTH COMMON
                                AND UNUSUAL.

MAY YOUR FOUNDATIONS EXHIBIT
THE STRENGTH OF OUR WISDOM AND KNOWLEDGE,
FOR WE HAVE WAITED A HUNDRED THOUSAND YEARS.

Rochdale College

is them
an   s
      i   l
      s   v
      t   e
hippies
put
 u. i
 tion

An invitation from the Association of Christians and Jews to attend a seminar took Duke and many other young Indians from across Canada to Banff. Duke and the others were angered by the format of the conference, as they listened to white archaeologists and anthropologists giving courses on Indian culture. Duke insisted that the best examples of Indian culture were sitting right in the room. The other Indians agreed, and out of that conference came the nucleus of a new organization, the Canadian Indian Youth Council.

The rebellious group went to Winnipeg, and there, Duke, Harold Cardinal and Tony Manadamin set up the CIYC with Tony as president and Duke as vice-president. The group developed Indian teach-ins, staged panel shows and sent speakers across Canada to deliver the Indian message to white university students.

Returning to Toronto, Duke discovered that the Thunderbird club had changed direction. When Duke suggested selling the club to interested buyers, John claimed the club for the people who were working in it. Duke sold the club—complete with its debt of one thousand dollars, to John, for one dollar. The club folded a year later.

While Duke was doing some work for the Royal Commission on Biculturalism and Bilingualism in 1965, he met Stewart Whittles and Ken McKay, who were developing the concept of the Company of Young Canadians and drawing up the necessary legislation for its inception. Duke was intrigued by the concept of highly idealistic young people forming an organization to promote social change.

In April of 1966, when the legislation was passed, Duke was hired by Bill McWhinney as a full-time officer at seven thousand five hundred dollars a year, plus expenses. Duke was hired as an assistant to Wilfred Pelletier, who, as Duke saw it, was the only person other than himself capable of developing an Indian program within the Company.

When I joined the Company, I wanted them to recognize the Indian constituency in Canada as a distinct region, which would hire Indian personnel and volunteers to direct projects in Indian communities. As it worked out, the company decided to treat Indians as part of the Canadian constituency, with provincial directors dealing with the Indian problems in their areas. I didn't agree with this policy because there wasn't anyone at that level really informed about the kinds of needs Indian people do have.

Duke tried to convince Pelletier that they could establish an exclusively Indian program if they backed up the demand with a threat of mass resignation if the rest of the Company didn't agree. Pelletier was reluctant to put his new job on the line.

A resolution was put before a full staff-meeting in Québec City, insisting that one of the associate directors of the Company should be an Indian. Ontario, Manitoba, and British Columbia backed the Indian members on the demand, but the rest of the Company shot it down.

Frustrated by Pelletier's reluctance to use his position to create pressure, Duke asked to be transferred to another office. Pelletier was fired and Duke was kicked upstairs as Program Officer for Evaluation of Projects Across Canada, but Duke was already reading the handwriting on the wall.

In my early days with the CYC, I had the naive belief that the government existed to help the people, that it was possible to change things in society and that the only problem with the government was that it didn't have the necessary information. I believed that when they got this information, they would immediately begin to solve the problems and that I would have a lot of influence and things would actually change. I believed the CYC was set up to help these changes come about in society.

It took a few years for me to realize that government isn't in the business of helping people or solving problems. Government is in the business of being the government. Whatever is expedient and efficient in allowing the government to stay the government, is what the government will put into effect. Anything that takes away from their ability to stay in power, they will reject. Whatever makes it easier for them to govern, they will appreciate.

In some ways, I made it easier for them to govern, because when I uncovered the problems before they became problems, they were able to reorganize themselves so they had a defense when the problem popped up in public. The reason I got invited to parties and government functions was that government officials wanted to pick my brains.

They would ask me all kinds of questions about what the CIYC was doing, or going to be doing next. To a lot of people, I represented an articulate path into the Indian mind. In the whole of Canada, there aren't more than a dozen Indians who can articulate Indian problems in English.

Duke found it fairly easy to handle the political manoeuvering that was going on within the Company. While others were being fired, he was getting raises. At one point, there was some serious consideration given to Duke becoming an Indian Member of Parliament.

There was a time, while I was with the Company, that I could have gone to the Yukon as Regional Director. The Yukon was under the Regional Director of British Columbia, but he wasn't really interested in doing anything up there because there were only fourteen thousand people.

The idea came up that I could be regional director there, so I took a trip up there. While I was there it became very clear to me that I could run for MP up there and win.

Politically, the situation was that the MP at the time, Eric Neilson, was disliked with a passion by the Liberals, but they had nobody in the Yukon who could challenge him.

But if the Indian people up there were to vote—they would hold the balance of power. I knew that I could go in there as Regional Director, hire five or six people, and with funds and travel expenses from the Company, I could cover the length and breadth of the Yukon and hire key people in every community. As a group, we could have caused all kinds of political hassles. Our job would have been to create social change, which would have given us credibility as a social voice.

When election time came around, this would be my political machine. We could have resigned and launched an up-front political campaign. I talked with influential people about it in a casual way. The response was very good from people like Martin O'Connell and the Liberal political organizers.

I didn't have any particular reason for abandoning the plan, but I began to get disillusioned with the whole political syndrome. I just decided that wasn't the trip for me. Politics as a lever for social change is not really useful. Social change comes about because peoples' minds and thinking change, not because there is a political platform or posture presented.

I didn't feel that even as an Indian Member in Parliament, that that would be where I would want to be for the rest of my life. If I got trapped in the political system, I wouldn't be able to function as I want to, or say what I have to say.

The 𝔈ompany of 𝔜oung 𝔈anadians is merely a 𝔊obernment organization providing a guaranteed annual wage for middle class radicals.

The ideas that Duke had about an Indian's chances of promoting social change with the political system, were reinforced when he met Len Marchand, the present Indian Member of Parliament. He met Marchand on a plane flight to an Indian conference in Edmonton.

As an Indian, he has turned his back on his own people and everything he should be doing for his people. He tries to make himself a reasonable facsimile of a white man and he operates that way. He tried to keep his Indian background out of his campaign, the same way Kennedy tried to keep his being Catholic from becoming an issue.

Jennifer Ray, a friend of the Prime Minister's was having this party, and I was invited. The PM was there, of course, and so were Chrétien, Turner, Macdonald, and a number of other people around Trudeau and in Trudeau's cabinet. I was treated in a very special way and introduced to all these people. I was dressed for a party and so was Trudeau and a lot of other very hip people.

But also in this group were the political types who weren't part of the new generation or the new order. They were dressed for a diplomatic function.

Len Marchand comes in and his mouth drops half a mile when he sees me and he asks me how I got to this party. He thought it was very special that he got invited. In he walks with his black tie trip—he could have come straight from a funeral—and his wife had on a long dress—the type they wear at diplomatic functions.

Both of them were standing unobtrusively in the background, and I was in the party: dancing with Jennifer Ray and carrying on. The PM is on one side doing discotheque kind of dancing, and there's music and dancing and all kind of groovy, creative-type people.

Outside the room where all of this is happening were the politicians, standing with drinks in their hands like a bunch of fence-posts. They couldn't drop their roles long enough to come and enjoy the party—but Trudeau could, and Chrétien and a few of the French-Canadian types could, but the white Anglo-saxons were standing way out there.

The vibrations I was getting from Len said he was afraid of me. He didn't know how I got to the party, or what my influence was with the people he wanted to influence, or how I was getting away with all this, being the kind of guy I am.

Here I go wheeling into the party, dressed like a playboy, acting like one, having a great time, fooling around with all the women and just carrying on. Everything in his background has told him

I used to think of becoming Canada's great Indian leader but Indians won't take that from me or anybody else that he has his place and to deviate from it is to lose out. Here his whole life has been a series of doing the right things so that he could arrive at the right place—only to run into me who has done all the wrong things and arrived there with more mobility and more influence, in a lot of ways.

Nobody introduced him when he walked in the door, but when I came in, Jennifer rushed up to me, grabbed me by the hand and pulled me across the room. She introduced me to the PM and to Chrétien and we were standing there chatting, and while all this is going on Len was coming in the door, unnoticed.

I don't think he has any potential as an Indian leader. He's an Uncle Tomahawk, a wishy-washy, namby-pamby liberal tokenist that the Indians in this country can do without.

Meanwhile the CIYC was well into its second year of operation with Duke as vice-president. The group functioned as a youthful more aggressive alternative to the staid NIC.

We could do all kinds of things on our own that the NIC didn't approve of. We got into red-power trips and made some very hard speeches, and did a lot of political posturing that the NIC was afraid to do because of the repercussions that might develop. There were too many old men on the NIC who stifled any real creative production.

As a youth group, we could talk about how Indians were being led down the garden path by the government. The older people wouldn't do this because they had too many historical ties with people in the Department of Indian Affairs, and even if they wanted to say what we were saying, they felt that they couldn't.

In its third year of operation, the CIYC moved to Ottawa and clashed head-on with the Department of Indian Affairs. The group's policy toward the Department was simple; get rid of it. Duke was more than willing to do what you have to do, and use what you have to use, to get what you want to get.

He learned that an all night vigil was being planned by the Student Union for Peace Action to protest Canada's complicity with the United States in the war in Vietnam. Duke saw a chance to get his own message across.

I just walked into the Department of Indian Affairs' Cultural Branch and went to work. I took some bristol-board and paints out of the cupboard, set them on the floor and started doing my signs protesting government imperialism against Indians. Nobody paid any attention to what I was doing. I just kept working away.

I didn't have any sticks, so I went to this church where the SUPA people were getting their thing together. They gave me the sticks and I stapled the signs right there. I guess they just didn't

believe me when I told them what I was going to do; they just laughed.

Sure enough, the next day the SUPA crowd sets up for their all night vigil on Parliament Hill. It was in the middle of winter and it was really cold. So me and three or four other guys show up just about the same time as the photographers from the newspapers.

Since I was a sign painter, my signs were really well-done with red paint and yellow shadows and borders and all that, and the SUPA signs were so bad you couldn't even read them. Anyway, the photographers come tearing up to us and flash away for their pictures and away they go, and I take off too.

The next day, the papers come and there we are, and the SUPA people aren't even in sight. Well, they were howling mad.

Someone at the Department of Indian affairs tipped off Director Robert Battle about what had happened. He couldn't help but laugh, but still, the government paying for anti-government demonstration signs was a little too much. The supply cupboards were locked from then on.

But Duke's attack on the Department of Indian Affairs was just beginning.

The Department of Indian Affairs is basically a nineteenth-century organization that is linear in its concepts and has a protestant ethic.

They say that the three main things an Indian should try to practice in life are: work, realizing the value of time and saving his money; all this at a time when even white society doesn't function like that any more.

They take an Indian who has qualities of creativity, spirituality and intuitiveness and they teach him to become a mechanic, to fix cars into which white society has built obsolescence.

I say disband the Department of Indian Affairs. Take their annual budget of two hundred million dollars and form a corporation—an Indian Development Corporation. Appoint an Indian board of directors, and let them hire people in a task-force way to do problem-solving.

What you'd have would be a crown corporation operating like the National Film Board or the Canadian Broadcasting Corporation. The Indian people would have the money to hire the best people in the world to solve the problems they found to be important. I know Martin O'Connell, parliamentary secretary to the Prime Minister is interested in the idea.

The CIYC, by co-ordinating youth activities across Canada, hoped to develop cultural esteem among Indians, and among whites, for Indians. But the old bugaboos of internal dissent, jealousy and power struggles affected this organization as well.

The organization didn't work because of the incompetence of the people who were running it. The stronger people, like myself, Harold Cardinal, Fred Kelly and Phil Fontaine, all wanted to be leader and didn't want the others to be leaders. So we'd come to a compromise and the most inept people would end up on top.

In its third year, I ran for president, but Fred Kelly got his group organized and a third inept person got in. I couldn't work under those conditions so I resigned. Now that there was nobody to compete with, the others resigned too, which left this incompetent holding the bag.

As the realization of Duke's concept of an Indian arm within the CYC became more remote, he began to size up his position. He began to feel he had been bought off by the government and effectively boxed in.

Duke saw that the government, with the creation of the CYC, had bought the leaders of most of Canada's radical youth and in effect had enclosed the middle-class radicals of the country into a manipulable group. He resigned from the Company a few months before the government crack-down and take-over became complete.

Unorganized groups can't be manipulated, but organized groups can be manipulated in the best interests of the government. The government wants to organize as many groups as it can, no matter how anti-establishment they might be. As long as they are organized, they can be manipulated by government. That is what government is concerned with.

Indians are unorganized—they have desires that have never been expressed in an organized way. Hippies, poets and artists are unorganized, so the government has no direct means of manipulation. If artists were organized into a union, then that group could make its demands on government and the government would say, "Alright, these are your demands; here are our demands; let's sit down and work out a bargain." Which means art would be compromised into accepting a mediocre level.

My basic tactical philosophy is, when in doubt, do the unexpected. In the CIYC I was fighting so hard to get into the leadership, that the last thing people expected was that I would get out of the fray. They thought they could defeat me and still use my talents and abilities. The whole thing was based, not on what the organization could do, but on the rivalry of the strong people involved. With me gone, it was no fun for Fred Kelly to compete with an incompetent. It was the same thing in the Thunderbird Club. All kinds of activity was generated by rivalry between myself and other people in the Club. When I sold the Club to them for a dollar and left, all those other activities folded up as well.

Duke returned to Toronto with the people who had supported him in the CIYC and formed an organization he named Indian Canada. He had learned that to function independently, you had to be financially independent. The group produced Indian arts and crafts, and silk-screened sweat shirts, put out its own newspaper and established its own club.

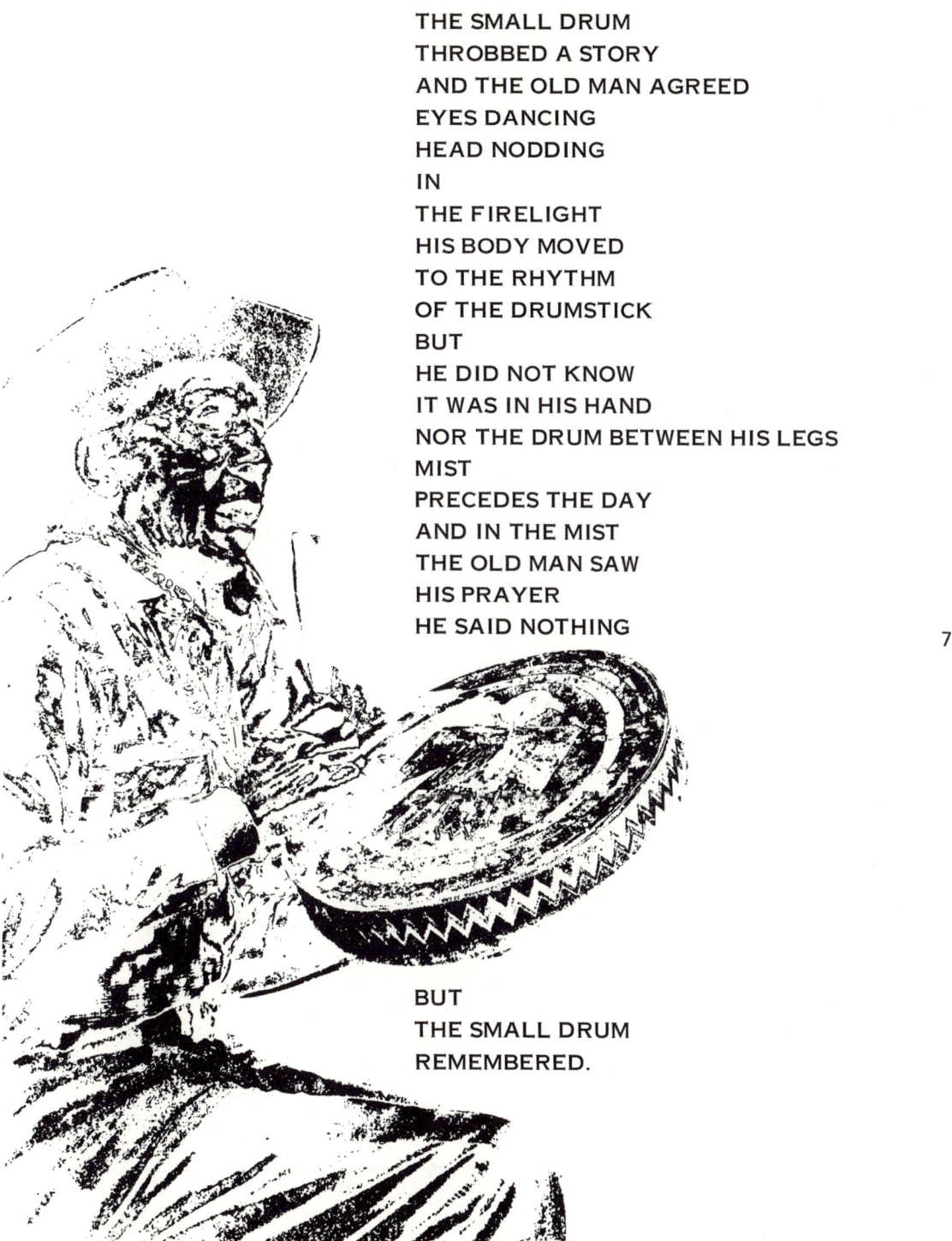

THE SMALL DRUM
THROBBED A STORY
AND THE OLD MAN AGREED
EYES DANCING
HEAD NODDING
IN
THE FIRELIGHT
HIS BODY MOVED
TO THE RHYTHM
OF THE DRUMSTICK
BUT
HE DID NOT KNOW
IT WAS IN HIS HAND
NOR THE DRUM BETWEEN HIS LEGS
MIST
PRECEDES THE DAY
AND IN THE MIST
THE OLD MAN SAW
HIS PRAYER
HE SAID NOTHING

BUT
THE SMALL DRUM
REMEMBERED.

*There is bannock in the morning
And old men with wrinkled faces.
There are black-haired mothers
With papooses on their backs.
There are young braves, straight and tall.
Their gentle laughter, singing and soft chatter
Is like a waterfall.*

I walk a barren desert
The scorching sun up in the sky,
The friendless burning sand
Beneath my tired feet.
Sometimes in the darkness
In the shadows of lonely dunes,
I hear a waterfall
And hang my sorrows for a moment
On its haunting, mocking call.
I climb a nameless mountain
While cumulus clouds
Hang heavy in the sky.
Foreboding deep dark crevasses
Slice open on every side.
And sometimes in the darkness
Of that eternal night
I hear a waterfall
And hang my hopes, my fears
A moment
On its haunting, mocking call.

I'm swimming in an ocean
White waves break monotonously
Across my aching brow.
Treacherous whirling pools
Drag my pain-wracked body down.
And sometimes in the grip
Of these milky murky depths
I hear the silvery tinkling
Of that glistening waterfall
And I hang my trials and tribulations
For a moment
On its haunting, mocking call.
There are Indian princesses
In the morning,
Beauty in buckskin—
Covered shawls.

They sing of teepees, chants, and drums
And herds of giant buffalo
Under a prairie sun.
They sing of horses' heads and feathered bonnets,
Of trees, and fields, and streams
And sometimes when I'm lonely
I hear them laughing in the misty, happy, splashing
Of that waterfall
And I hang all my worldly labours and recline in dreaming
On its haunting, mocking call.

In 1968, Indian Canada was asked to form a dance troupe to tour Mexico during the Olympics. Duke revived the old Thunderbird Dancers and with nine hundred dollars from the Folk Arts Council they made costumes for twelve girls and twelve men.

It was in Mexico that Duke had his own sense of cultural esteem boosted. Duke discovered that Mexicans, although they have little use for their own Indian people, have a respect for the "noble savage" that borders on the romantic.

When I got off the plane in Mexico, for the first time in my life I didn't feel like a minority. Everybody looked like an Indian—and I'd never had that kind of feeling before.

There was an even greater contact with his Indian identity in the City of the Gods. Here he reached the end of his search for identity.

When we visited the City of the Gods, I wasn't prepared for what I found. The first thing that impressed me was the sheer size of the ruins. You could stack them up against the Toronto-Dominion Centre without blushing. The layout stretched for miles. It took all day just to wander around them.

But the real experience for me was the Temple to the Sun. I had a real sense of joy, being there. I noticed a number of Mexican Indians camped at the base of the pyramid. They looked as if they had travelled a long way to get there and were in no hurry to go home. They were pilgrims, not tourists. Then I climbed to the top of the Pyramid to the Sun. There was a great blue expanse of sky without a cloud in it and you could see for miles.

While I was standing there, I felt a real exhilaration, a tremendous sense of power. I turned to an Indian friend who had climbed with me, and said:

"This is it. We're home."

For a few minutes, it really felt that way. All kinds of things were rushing through my head. I felt I had been here before in another time, as a priest, maybe. The fact that things had happened so that I ended up four thousand miles from my home on the top of this pyramid has mystical implications. It wasn't an accident that I was here. Somehow or other, a path had been created to get me here. It was while I was there that I knew what it meant to be together. I really knew, then, what it was about— what I was about, as an Indian.

You could see what it must have been like when this city bustled with a million people. This is where they worshipped their gods, up on top of a pyramid, not in some gloomy cathedral with stained glass windows filtering the light onto dark stone statues.

These people worshipped their gods outside, and I can understand why. On the top of the pyramid, looking up at the sky, you can feel a sense of the omnipotent. Not only can you feel greatness in terms of gods, but you can also see the results of your own work spread out before you. There it is. There's man, and there's God. No wonder people who worship in churches feel so small in comparison to their god.

At the time, I thought to myself, that if I could only bring the Indian leadership of Canada down here, to experience the tremendous work that the Indian people have achieved, they would come back to Canada and forget their petty differences and difficulties and the political game-playing which is the greatest barrier to the development of Indian culture in Canada. Few Canadian Indians have ever seen anything of merit that they could identify with, as being a product of the Indian personality.

I didn't feel any despair over the fact that this great city was a ruin. At another level, I felt that here was the work of the body—these people had gone to the ultimate in terms of their physical extensions of themselves. We no longer have to put up pyramids to the sun and to the moon.

Like thousands of visitors before him, Duke was impressed with the stark contrasts in Mexican life. He was surprised by the friendly and happy attitudes of the people in spite of the obvious evidence of a fascist militarist government. He had found a country that contained at least as many contradictions as he himself did.

The thing that struck me first was the poverty. In Canada we tend to hide our poverty, but in Mexico the poverty is all around, and the rich live in ghettos. There are four distinct cultures evident in Mexico—the Indian, the Spanish, the Indian-Spanish, and the North American.

The country is almost a fascist state. When I was there the army was very evident. A couple of days before I arrived they had had riots and they had machine-gunned six hundred demonstrators in the main square. We had an armed guard on the bus with us at all times. The gate to the compound where we lived was guarded by a very high fence. Inside this compound, there were all kinds of food and everything you could want, but outside those gates was the worst kind of poverty. You couldn't walk down the street without running into beggars.

The Mexicans were very friendly and very happy. You didn't feel the tension and uptightness that you feel here. In Mexico, every house is a fortress and the people protect themselves in this fortress. In Canada we can live in our houses without locks and keys, but we have to walk around in our body fortresses. Our fortress is our body and our defense against physiological aggression.

The ordinary people are very culturally oriented—the theatre arts and the dance are really very respectable. They have a great deal of enthusiasm for that part of their life. In Canada, it doesn't matter how good you are, if you get clapping out of the audience, you are lucky, but Mexicans whoop and holler and yell "Bravo" and "encore" and give standing ovations. It happens at every performance.

The Mexican people have a fondness and a respect for what they call Indios—the native, original people—almost a mystical fascination with Indian people. They have an idea of Indians from the north as a romantic noble savage, but they are not very happy with their own Indian people. If you can't read and write, you're an Indian. If you can, you're a Mexican.

We, as Canadians, were very well received with lots of curtain calls and bravos, but the particular American troupe that was there had learned some

Mexican dances. When they got up to do their performance, they were literally chased right off the stage. The audience was insulted that gringos would try to do their national dances—and do them badly at that. Mexican audiences are like that—if they don't like you they are liable to kill you.

I wasn't there long enough to find out if I could live in Mexico, but I doubt it. I don't know that I could really relate to the Mexican people. I was something of an oddity while I was there. I looked like they did, but I was obviously a Canadian. Since they work on the basis that all Canadians are rich, I was given a great deal of deference.

I didn't get the feeling that I could walk off the plane and become part of their world. I was really glad to be back in Canada. The trees, the mountains, the lakes and the rivers are home. I didn't feel any rapport with the palm tree or the cactus, or the desert.

The final contrast Duke noticed left a very deep impression. From it came one of his best poems.

I saw this old woman walking down the road with this great stack of wood on her back. At the time I thought, in terms of endurance and what she had to go through to do that, she deserves the gold medal, rather than these guys over at the Olympic Coliseum who were running around the track in ten seconds. Right outside the gates are the people who really deserve the medals, in terms of the effort they have to expend just to survive.

They spend millions of dollars building coliseums and great public buildings so they can put on these games, and half of Mexico is starving to death.

Old woman in the field
Bent low, immobile, still.
What thoughts tumble about
Behind those sad, black eyes
That have not felt the moist
Edges and wet bodies of heart-broken tears
Since the hunger pangs of transgression
And broken promises melted away with the passing years?
What language does the stream of consciousness employ?
Is it sound, or words, or mists of past reflections,
Hastily snatched before the precious
Breath of life forsakes you entirely?

No time now old woman
For multiplication-tables and essays.
No time now for politics and religion.
No time now for polite conversation.
How close you are to the earth,
How low you're bent.
In the lengthening shadows
You appear to be another stone
On the bare horizon,
And the bright sun of your youth
Has faded softly behind you
So that now the rays only
Reflect your image across the naked desert.
And what of you?
Will you slip below the surface
Of my perception,
And slip away from my understanding
And stand in the darkness?
Old woman, I know who you are.
I know this barren waste land
Upon which I stand
Was once a forest.

And you, old woman,
Had life and beauty,
Energy and passion,
Love and abundance,
Freedom, and chatter with the gods.
Birch trees cried, "Here, take my bark
That you may sleep in my arms."
And the great creatures of the forests
Dropped their fur clothing and said
"Let my warmth be your warmth,
Make a pillow for your feet."
And the birds swooped down
And laid their finest plumage at your feet
And bade you wear them.
For you were their child.
Their brown, golden child,
Who sang their praises and danced their dance.
No, your eyes have not harboured tears,
But your body carried the burden
Of sorrow, and the weight of treachery.
For others came, pale helpless souls.
And your arms encircled them,
And your golden mouth kissed them.
This was your youth, old woman,
Bent so low.

Where are they now,
After they cut down your beloved forest,
And slaughtered your animal brothers,
And tore the wings from your bright birds,
And ground your mountains into dust?
Did they leave you anything at all,
Except pain, and misery, and hunger?
What thoughts have you,
What last word before you give up
Your spirit to eternity?
Did they leave you even that
One word
One thought
To take with you to the last hunting-ground
Love?

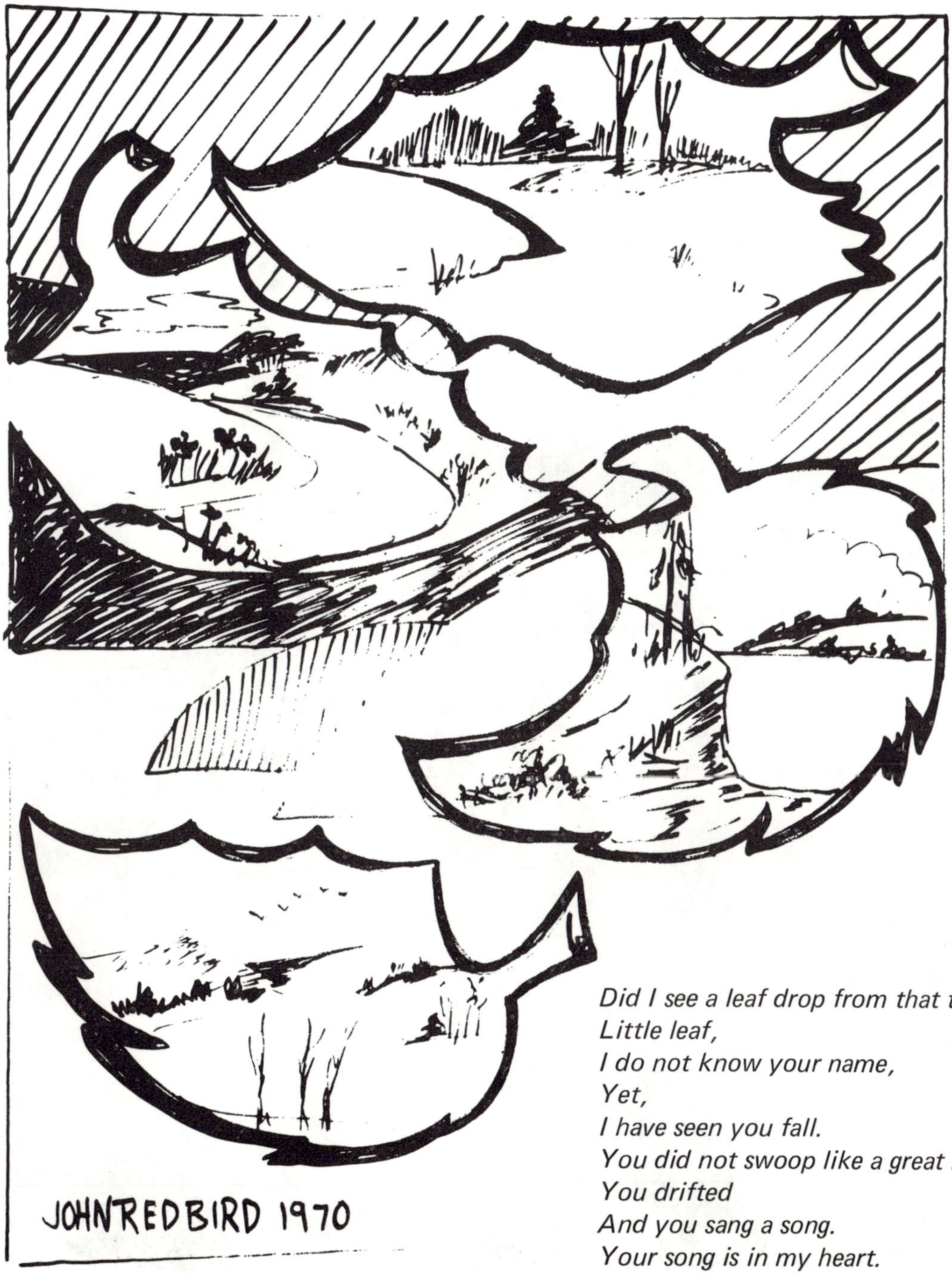

Did I see a leaf drop from that tree?
Little leaf,
I do not know your name,
Yet,
I have seen you fall.
You did not swoop like a great hawk.
You drifted
And you sang a song.
Your song is in my heart.

I Know What Kind Of World I Live In

I know that the society I live in is not geared to love. The tree of hatred carries the crucified remains of every martyr that ever dared advance the cause of love. Every man that ever got up and talked about love and beauty has been shot down. When I see Mahatma Ghandi, Christ and practically every other man who had an ideal, from Socrates onward, killed by the establishment—this tells me what kind of a world I live in.

In my last ten years in North America, I've seen Martin Luther King, Bobby Kennedy and John F. Kennedy killed because they tried to respond to something greater than money and power.

Duke returned to Toronto and Indian Canada, with the taste of revolution as a reality still in his mouth. Up to now, Duke had been thinking in terms of influencing people with ideas, of using existing government and media channels to promote change for the Canadian Indian, but it became very obvious that others were willing to take it several steps further—into armed revolution if necessary.

Tony Antoine, of the Native Alliance for Red Power, came out from Vancouver. They talked seriously about what would be involved in a guerilla or military approach to solving their problems. Duke had already been approached by separatists.

There were separatists from French Canada who talked to me about involving Indians with their movement in Quebec, and right across Canada for that matter. When they want to raise money, they go out and rob banks, and they have ways and means of getting guns, dynamite and ammunition together. I had a number of meetings in Montreal with these separatist types of revolutionaries. They were trying to feel me out as to how serious I was as a red-power-type leader.

At the time, the FLQ and the separatists seemed to be one and the same. I couldn't name these people if I wanted to, because I wasn't interested enough in what they were doing. Besides, I was angry about what the Union Nationale had done to the Indians and the Eskimos. Before the Union Nationale took over, they were in a kind of separatist bag themselves, but when they took power in Quebec they stepped in and made all these Indians learn French.

The Indians were English-speaking. They had gone from speaking Indian to English, and now they had to learn French. Not only that, but they moved whole villages of Indians from the north of the province to the south, nearer the copper mines.

So when these guys got talking about how they were going to help Quebec by separating, and breaking down the establishment, I got really uptight because I could see what would happen to the Indians if these guys ever took power. They'd be harder on us than the present establishment is. I told them that, but that just made them try all the harder to convince me. I used to go around to the Bistro and the Spanish Club in Montreal where the separatists were hanging out. They wanted the Indians as allies, but there was no way they were going to get them if they didn't let Indians have their own language and do their own thing.

When Antoine left, a Chinese fellow contacted me and said he represented an oriental marxist organization and had been involved with the Student Union for Peace Action. We had a long discussion about SUPA.

A few days later, a couple of guys from Detroit, who called themselves Black Nationalists, showed up. They were connected with the Black Panthers. They came over expressly to talk to me about the possibility of linking up ideologically, if not functionally, with what they were doing in the United States. They said there were training programs available, so that a revolutionary type of activity could get started in Toronto.

Another group that talked to me in Montreal was a right wing up-with-people group. They were John Bircher types that put out a magazine called Canada Month, and there was another guy that put out a newspaper called En Ville. These guys were pro-English.

I get a call from the newspaper guy who says he's looking for young Indians to train as reporters and he wants me to get involved. He's saying things like: "We're trying to weed out the cancer in this society, like homosexuality and incest." And he goes on this weird sex trip—every second word was faggot and so on: and this is a guy who runs a newspaper backed by ads from Montreal businesses.

I tried to tell him that, as a group, Indians don't think you have to go to church to get married. The more I tried to explain, the more fanatical he became about immorality and sleeping around and all that.

I was listening to what they had to say, and what I picked up from both the separatists and the black nationalists was that the Indians would be the little brown brothers of these big brothers. It was obvious that when the revolution was over, the Indian would still just be a little brown brother, and I didn't like that idea.

Because our numbers were so small, compared to the groups that were really getting involved in the revolution, the only way the Indians could be effective in an organization like that would be if there were a pan-Indian movement in South America as well as North America. That would bring our numbers up to around the two hundred million mark.

Well, then it occurred to me that in order to develop a pan-Indian movement I would have to start simultaneous revolutions in about a dozen Latin American countries as well as the US and Canada. That alone would be several lifetimes' work, even if it were possible, and at the time, I thought it was impossible.

The guy at Canada Month had the same kind of trip. He was all very impressed with my credentials and everything, but he was on a white-power trip. He was saying that white men can help save the Indian and it was certainly good to see someone like myself discard the savage ways of my ancestors and come into white society.

I sat around and listened to these guys, and let them do their trip. The whole Moral Rearmament group have to be as much hypocrites as the revolutionaries—the FLQ.

Those two groups could get along just fine—they are one and the same in so many ways. The far right and the far left both want to accomplish the same things. The right says take Quebec off the back of the rest of Canada and let them stew in their own poverty. The left says we want to separate.

I don't think the action and reaction of revolution will be the most powerful influencing factor in improving the Indian's life in the modern world. It's how people are going to react to the technological and sociological re-structuring of society that's beginning now, that will determine the type of revolution or evolution that will take place. There is no way to predict what future-shock is going to do to populations in North and South America. It was just too early to make those kinds of commitments.

The Maoist that came to see me—I think what he wanted basically, was to have Indians, who move freely back and forth across the American border, affiliated with his group. They were planning some kind of underground railroad for draft-dodgers.

I explained to them that I had no desire to be the little brown brother of either the black man or the yellow man. They claim that they will be free when we are free, but that's impossible. At least the way we have it now, we are beginning to learn the psychology of the white man and how to deal with him. But Christ, to have to learn the whole trip over again to become compatible with the yellow man or the black man just isn't worth it. I say let's stick to what we know about.

When I was going to universities and high schools, a lot of kids got really uptight because I wasn't making statements about taking up guns and going out to fight. I was telling them, "Don't you understand that if we did that we'd be wiped out?—that they'd just put us against the wall and shoot us down?"

"Oh, no," they'd say, "Not in a democratic society. The government can't do that. Look at the FLQ. They blew up a few mail boxes and they got all kinds of help, and now people are looking at Quebec."

"They're looking at Quebec all right," I'd tell them, "But when you become a threat to the government, the government will kill you. And there's no qualification, they have the power and they'll do it."

Well it really didn't hit them with an impact until yesterday, when the War Measures Act was invoked. I don't think that the FLQ and the guys I knew in it really believed the government could just take complete power and move in troops.

You see that's where a lot of people are naive about the world we live in and its governments. The government can do anything it wants to do, and public opinion can do little to stop it. I don't think there is ever an emergency that warrants taking that kind of power unless you are attacked by foreign nations. The Liberal government has had since 1962 to figure out the kind of legislation they needed to handle this kind of an eventuality, and they could have done something more realistic and more democratic.

Duke's conviction that pyramid organizations simply weren't effective in terms of social change was growing stronger. He quit the CIYC and the organization folded. He had thought that group action gave him a better chance to get his ideas into action, but experience was teaching him that he might be better off on his own. He was learning that the establishment had ways of dealing with groups to maintain the status quo.

If you take on the establishment head-on, you are just indicating to them ways of making better chains for you. If you form a conventional organization, they react immediately and create a counter-organization: like the way they controlled change through the CYC. To meet them head-on is just suicide.

What you have to do is approach the whole thing obliquely. You have to change people's ideas, and the only way you can do that is through the media. You have to attack on a cultural rather than a political level.

I figured if I was going to have any real power in changing the status quo I would have to re-direct the forces I had going for myself toward the media, and the indications are that the choice was the right one. I'm able to function in the media and gain access for a revolutionary kind of thing, but I think of myself more as an evolutionist than a revolutionary because the social evolution in North America is eventually going to favour the Indian.

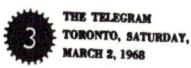

THE TELEGRAM
TORONTO, SATURDAY,
MARCH 2, 1968
Pages 35-48

Weekend/Showcase

McGuinness
D'Eaubonne
Brandy
The best for less.

RED POWER

It's the rallying call for Canada's restless young braves. It's an echo of Black Power, but don't be alarmed, it doesn't mean Kill Whitey or Burn, Baby, Burn. It means, in simplest terms, cultural persuasion

By BARBARA KLICH

"Red power will be the saving force in the coming years."

Duke Redbird is a 28-year-old Canadian Indian, who writes radio scripts for the CBC, writes and produces plays for the Toronto scene, and is a firm, fervent believer in the coming of age of his people.

"The white man has to realize that the Indian is there, right there in the cities. There are at least 8,000 Indians in Toronto now and the old stereotype of the no-good, drunken, Indian bum is just a lot of nonsense. The Indian culture will be the real key to the Indian's success in the future and to the white man's happiness as well."

As well as a writer, and a philosopher, this handsome young man is the director of the recently-opened Indian Canada Centre on Grenville st.

"We want this to be a place for the Indian writers, actors, and poets to come and talk about our culture and to produce the kind of things that should have been created and produced years ago."

The centre is a basement room near Ward Price Auctioneers. It has 2,500 square feet of space for the writers and actors to mill around, or to rehearse their works. The walls are brightened here and there with Indian art, half traditional and half modern, and a bear skin rug covers part of the floor. The centre is not there as a stepping stone for the Indian coming into the city, but rather a meeting spot for the Indian who wants to be able to identify with his traditions and his culture.

Duke feels that the cultural bet is the best one to play in trying to bring the Canadian Indian as a person into proper focus.

"I am not a protest type; perhaps, I could be called an aggressive pacifist, but I really feel that we can achieve more through our culture than we can through protests. We have to take a positive approach to the problems of our people. And, now the time is ripe. The return of the Red Man is now . . . you see this trend in magazines, on radio, in television. Even McLuhan has stated that the tribal society will be the electronic-age society. As Indians, we are well equipped to face that kind of society and that kind of future."

Duke has not always felt that confidence about his future. He was raised in a series of foster homes in the Niagara Peninsula and left school when he was 16. He has some bitter thoughts about his people and the pressures imposed on them by the white race.

"The Indian people were really treated in much the same way as the Jews were treated in the Nazi regime. They were not allowed to practice their religion, speak their own languages, live in their own traditional ways. Even today, in some of the church-operated schools, the Indian kids are given poor foods, they are beaten; homosexuality is ram-

pant in these schools; the freedoms the white man expects as his birthright in Canada are denied the Indian."

Can you equate the problems of the Indian in Canada with those of the Negro in the United States. No, says Redbird, early North American treatment of the Indians was far more harsh than that meted out to the Negroes.

"They slaughtered our people, at least in the States. The Negro was made a slave and given a chance to live. Our education was denied us, our rights, everything that should have been ours."

The Indian Canada Centre wants to right some of these long-lived wrongs and Duke feels we are near the time in history when a distinctly Indian corps of writers and actors will emerge. He feels that the Indian has no James Baldwin, no Jackie Robinson, no significant symbol.

"But, we have so much more than the Negro . . . we have our own language, which he doesn't have, we have a religion, we have Indian music . . . all of these things and we will bring them to the attention of the whites."

In their favor, according to Duke, is the fact that over 60 percent of Canada's Indians are now under 25. They are young, alive, vitally interested in their world and not as complacent as their parents had been.

"The old Indian and the young as well, identified with nature around him . . . he adapted to his environment. The white man identifies with the material things around him . . . his world is a rotting, rusting, thing and he rusts with it. Life is different to an Indian and when the Government stepped in and gave welfare — this source of return replaced the bounty of nature the Indian had known. The Indian think in terms of the moon, the stars, the sun . . . but this doesn't mean he is lazy. His has been a different world. His life was governed by his place in the tribal community. When he comes to an urban centre he feels the same things as he always did, but the other people react in a different manner."

Some of the things the Indian identifies with are his musical instruments and traditions and Duke mentioned that Indian Canada holds Sunday dances where the drums, the mouth bow, and shells are used for background music.

"You see, ours has been a culture based on nature . . . not on sanctuaries where you hide in the dark and mutter a prayer but where you stand on a hill and talk to your God; ours has been a culture of wandering and accepting the environment, not one of cities and buildings. Somehow, through our centre we will bring this culture to the attention of the white and awaken the level of the Indian consciousness in the public."

Working with Duke in his endeavors are his brother, John, a painter and wood carver, and Terry LaValley, who works with the Company of Young Canadians.

Like the wind that blows
The restless leaves of autumn
From north and south
From east and west
Four winds blow across this land
They're called the winds of change
And they blow upon the Indian breast.

They came . . .

They came from garden river and oshweken
They came from odanak and caughnawaga
They came from many places
With strange and common names
The cree, blackfoot, odawa, mohawk,
The chippewa, abeniki, ojibway, and sioux,
The Indian sons and daughters.

And there, beneath the mountain-top
In the shadow of eternal rock
The four winds of change
Fanned an inward fire
From the glowing coals of hope
That burn within the Indian heart
Of the Indian sons and daughters.

And these four winds
That blow from each direction
Have left a fire of hope
Within their hearts
That this Indian nation
Shall not be scattered
Like the restless leaves of autumn.

Duke moved himself and his family into an apartment in Rochdale College. Although he was living on the seventeenth floor—where the Institute for Indian Research was located—he wasn't formally attached to the organization. He hoped he could revive the old Thunderbird newspaper and set up seminars on Indian culture.

He appeared on a local television show and was introduced as a "resource person" from the Indian Institute at Rochdale. Although Duke denied he was connected with the organization, Wilfred Pelletier, who was operating the institute, was watching the show. He began spreading the word that Duke was trying to take over and that as long as Duke was around, the Institute would be denied government funds.

Duke, meanwhile, had received an offer from the World University Service organization to do a cross-Canada speaking tour. He jumped at the chance.

> The thing I liked doing best was lecturing at universities. I have lectured on psychology, anthropology, archaeology, sociology, economics, history and drama. All of these things can be appreciated from an Indian point of view and they come out looking quite different from the way the white man sees them.

When he returned from the tour, he found Pelletier had organized his opposition to Duke's presence in Rochdale. He repeatedly asked Duke to attend meetings to answer the "rumours" that were circulating about him. Pelletier then organized a petition asking that Duke be expelled from Rochdale. Six people signed it.

> **Wilfred kept setting up these meetings and asking me to come—like a prisoner at an inquisition—and defend myself. I just told him to fuck off. I've got nothing to be defensive about. So I just packed up my family and left. Who needs the hassle? Wilfred's brother, Tommy, decided to leave with me.**

Now thoroughly convinced that organizations, as such, were a poor outlet for his message, Duke turned to his old love, the mass media. Since his first television appearance in 1964, Duke had been on dozens of radio and television programs. As an Indian spokesman, he had done shows with *Take Thirty, Pierre Berton, Perry's Probe, Elwood Glover, The Morning After,* and the *National News.*

In 1968, he began appearing in dramatic roles. His first dramatic appearance was as a dancer in *The Forest Ranger* series. This led to a small part in *Quentin Jurgens,* and *McQueen,* and a major role in *Rainbow Country* which began in 1970.

He appeared in three documentaries, *Indian Dialogue, Pow Wow at Duck Lake,* and *Saul Alinski Goes to War*, before writing a script and doing the commentary for a Film Canada production called *Indian Pow Wow*, and a poetry reading for the Tommy Hunter Show.

Duke then moved to Ottawa and started working on a few projects of his own. He got a contract with the National Film Board to do a satirical film based on Charlie Squash—a cartoon character Duke had created for the Thunderbird newspaper. The film was sold by the NFB to Columbia pictures and was released in the summer of 1970 in theatres across the country.

In September, he moved back to Toronto and was called by Herb Whittaker to act as a consultant for the Toronto production of the *Ecstasy of Rita Joe.* Duke was intrigued by his first contact with legitimate theatre and decided to try out for a part. He got the lead role of Jamie Paul. A new door was opening.

While Duke was involved with all of these radio, television and stage productions, he was learning. His quick and observant mind absorbed an enormous amount of information on staging, lighting, and dramatic production in general. A few weeks later, he was lecturing on drama to the theatre arts drama class at Glendon College, Toronto.

While the showbusiness door was opening, another door was closing. Duke and Elaine split up.

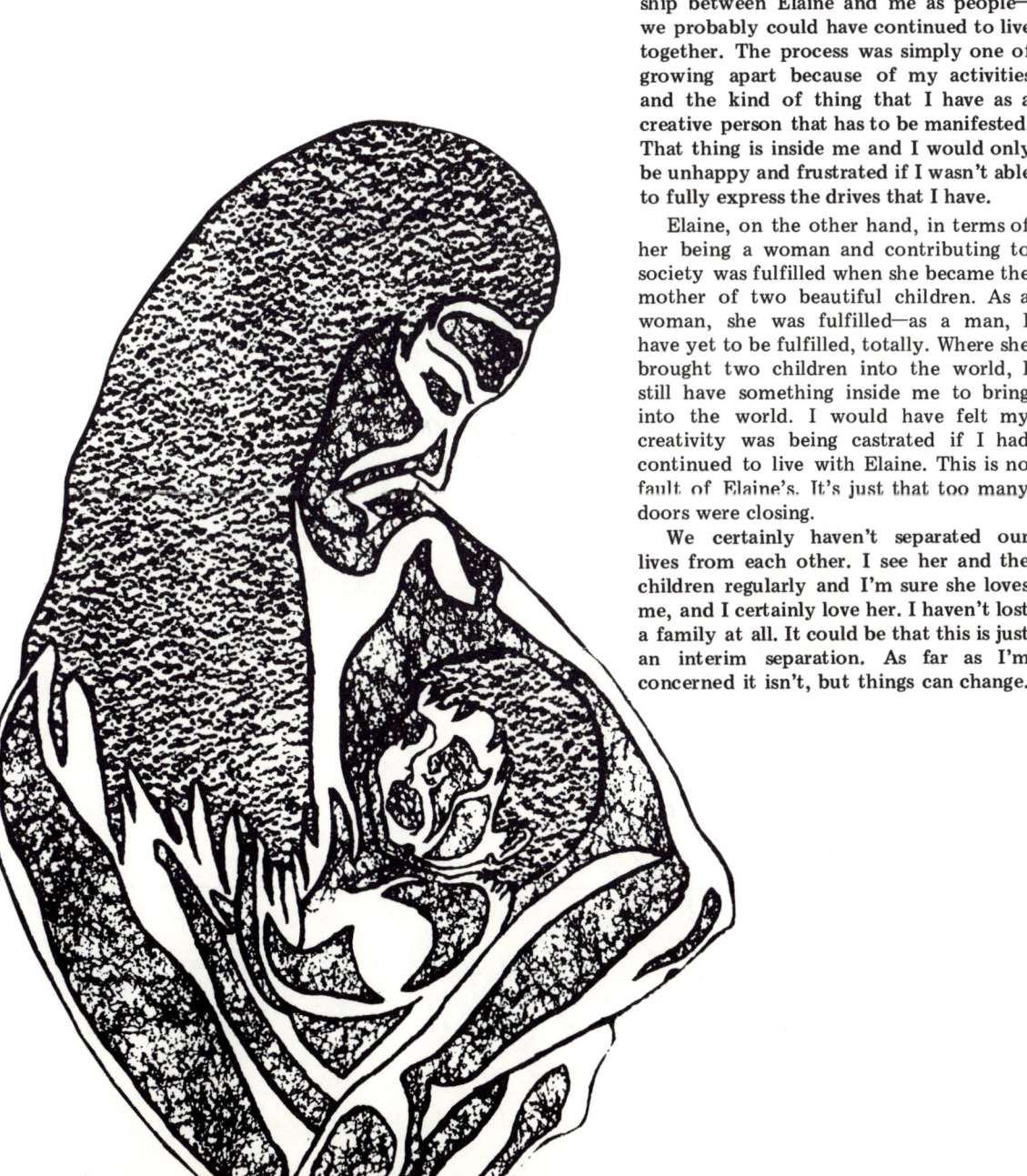

It wasn't a breakdown in the relationship between Elaine and me as people—we probably could have continued to live together. The process was simply one of growing apart because of my activities and the kind of thing that I have as a creative person that has to be manifested. That thing is inside me and I would only be unhappy and frustrated if I wasn't able to fully express the drives that I have.

Elaine, on the other hand, in terms of her being a woman and contributing to society was fulfilled when she became the mother of two beautiful children. As a woman, she was fulfilled—as a man, I have yet to be fulfilled, totally. Where she brought two children into the world, I still have something inside me to bring into the world. I would have felt my creativity was being castrated if I had continued to live with Elaine. This is no fault of Elaine's. It's just that too many doors were closing.

We certainly haven't separated our lives from each other. I see her and the children regularly and I'm sure she loves me, and I certainly love her. I haven't lost a family at all. It could be that this is just an interim separation. As far as I'm concerned it isn't, but things can change.

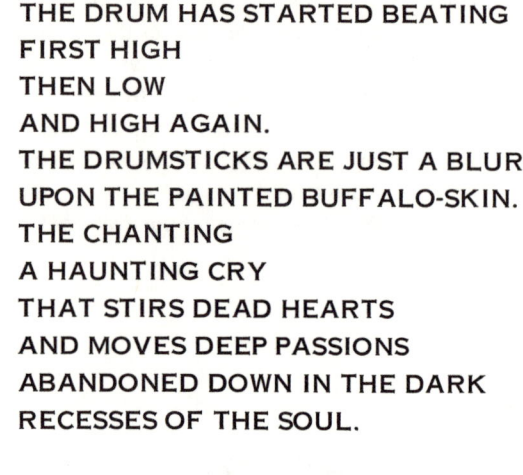

THE DRUM HAS STARTED BEATING
FIRST HIGH
THEN LOW
AND HIGH AGAIN.
THE DRUMSTICKS ARE JUST A BLUR
UPON THE PAINTED BUFFALO-SKIN.
THE CHANTING
A HAUNTING CRY
THAT STIRS DEAD HEARTS
AND MOVES DEEP PASSIONS
ABANDONED DOWN IN THE DARK
RECESSES OF THE SOUL.

I CLOSE MY EYES AND DARKNESS HAS DISAPPEARED
COLOUR FLOW IS EVERYWHERE
LEAPING AND BOUNDING
LAUGHING AND SWIRLING
RISING AND FALLING
SPINNING AND CURLING
RHYTHMICALLY AND SYMMETRICALLY
THE CHANT AND THE DRUM.

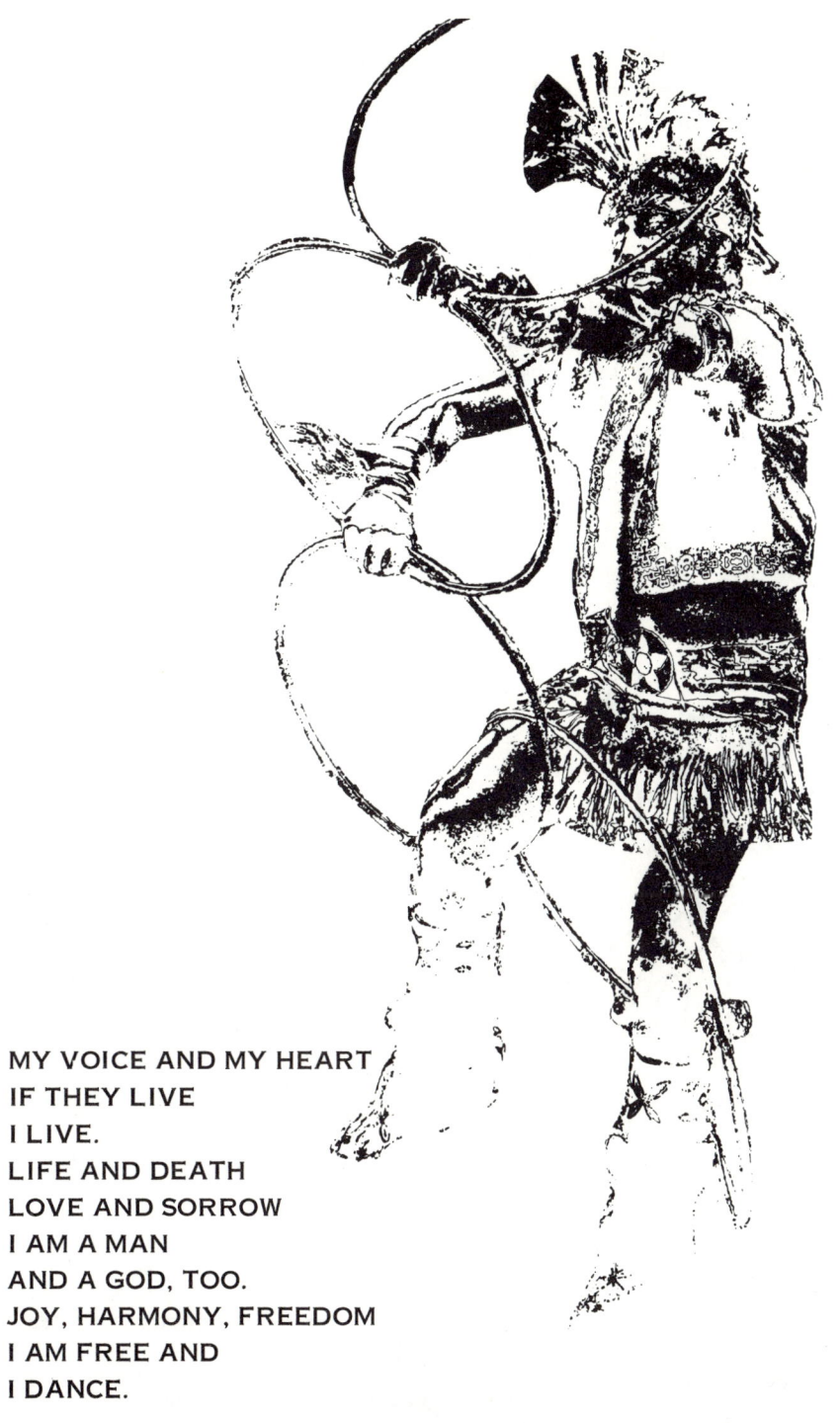

MY VOICE AND MY HEART
IF THEY LIVE
I LIVE.
LIFE AND DEATH
LOVE AND SORROW
I AM A MAN
AND A GOD, TOO.
JOY, HARMONY, FREEDOM
I AM FREE AND
I DANCE.

The biggest single change I noticed in Duke after we began working together, was his concern and involvement with cybernetics, computers and the total-systems technology. He first became interested in these ideas when Bob Olivero, Director of Administration of the Company of Young Canadians, explained some of the basic principles to him. When he met George Yost, an architect and MIT graduate, of Project Planners in Toronto, his interest was fanned into flames. He began to explore the connection between the developing science of cybernetics and the tribal systems of the Canadian Indians.

The idea developed rapidly, and although it was obvious enough to Duke, communicating that idea to someone else was something different. Strangely enough, the university community picked up on the idea first. During the World University Service tour, Duke hit almost every campus in the country with his ideas about the cybernetic world being a direct development of tribal culture. His audiences were amazed, sceptical, but definitely interested.

"Cybernetics" comes from the Greek word "cyber," which is the rudder of a ship, or the person who mans the rudder. When you travel in a boat you start toward a goal, but because of the variables of wind and waves, you can't head for your destination in a straight line, so you are constantly correcting your course in terms of the variables. In English, the word was first applied to torpedoes that followed their targets by means of a correctional mechanism that re-directed them in relation to the target.

Indian societies were basically cybernetic in their problem-solving. Any problem was approached in a task-force way. When the tribe was trading, the best merchant in the tribe would be leader for that period of time. When the trading was over and they needed a negotiator, the person who was the best statesman became the leader. In time of war, the best warrior would become the leader of the group. This is the kind of participatory democracy that the Indians had at the time the white man came.

Today the Western European is creating a cybernetic society because of the influence of the North American continent. This influence caused him to develop a consumer-oriented pattern, rather than the European pattern based on producing. The collective unconscious of North America appears to be pointed in that direction.

The Western European man has created a physical and social superstructure in the form of a labyrinth, which people are introduced to when they are born and have to search their way through over a lifetime. It was and is, a real structure. The cities, towns, social patterns, politics, culture, religion, and the economics of Western Europe were built in a chaotic labyrinthine fashion. Within that structure, people were born, lived, and died without ever knowing a sense of freedom, peace, or enlightenment.

When he came to North America, he discovered that that structure did not exist here, so in the name of civilization, he set about building it as quickly as possible—but the structures that had been developed in Western Europe didn't fit into the gestalt of the North American continent. As a result, North Americans were, and are, misfits in terms of European culture. The desire to create a maze or labyrinth existed in the Western Europeans who came to North America, but here they found themselves creating both an entrance and an exit for the system—while the European structure is a closed system.

In North America, the nature of the continent is such that order, of a haphazard kind, had been achieved out of a desire to create a counterpart of the European labyrinth. The difference here, is that because of the different kind of consciousness on this continent, a different kind of superstructure has been created. A superstructure that has, built within it, a self-correctional or change process that is the cybernetic quality of North American consciousness.

The difference between the two cultures is that where the European system is static and very difficult to change, the North American structures are cybernetic or evolving, with a built-in, dynamic, ever-changing quality. That is the difference between Western Europeans and North Americans.

The Europeans arrived in North America at the time of the British, French, and German colonial empires. They really believed that they had discovered all of the rules that should govern society and that things shouldn't be done outside those rules. Tradition had set in to such a degree that it was the foundation on which everything operated, and they wanted to leave that alone, but in North America, people don't accept that what went on before is necessarily the correct way of doing things. In North America, the idea is that as soon as you know how to do something, that something is obsolete. In Western Europe, when you know how to do something, they believe you have gained your freedom.

The cybernetic process operates on other levels too. Look at it in terms of how decisions are reached among a group of people. If your culture is such that you believe the least admirable trait in an individual is standing on principle, and the most admirable is that of compromise, then you arrive at a consensus quickly—because a person gains status from his ability to compromise with another point of view.

In order to come to a decision, each person listens to the point of view of all the others, and each person modifies his stand in light of what has been said. As opposed to the white man's way of doing things, where one man stands up and says, "I don't give a damn what you want, but I admire you for sticking to your principles and not giving in."

When you have a whole people operating at a compromise level, an agreement is inevitable. Indians have even created the word OK, which signifies an area of agreement. The function of an Indian society is such that data is being taken in by every person in the group and fed back into the group, which enables them to function in a cybernetic manner.

There was no need to create books because each situation was handled at face value, with known precedent being just one of many factors considered. There was no need for legislation, judges, magistrates and formal institutions.

At the tribal level the people functioned as a group, but like a flock of geese flying in formation, each individual had to continually correct himself to maintain the pattern—just as the v-formation of geese changes from second to second but maintains its basic shape. From the outside, it appears to maintain a specific formation, but in precise terms, that formation is continually changing. The tribal group is a continuously modulating group.

The movement in present day society toward an electronic, computerized, total systems, cybernetic, technological society is a movement toward becoming Indian in North America, because Indians have always lived in a cybernetic kind of world. Before the white man came, Indians knew that every blade of grass, every tree, had a spiritual counterpart that had you under surveillance at all times, and you had to be very careful not to offend those spirits. When we develop electronic surveillance of everyone, it will amount to the same thing.

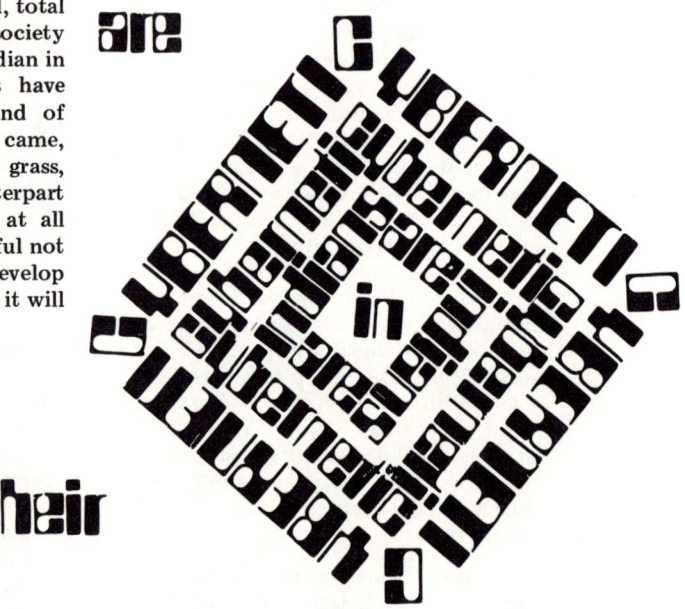

INDIANS are CYBERNETIC in their PROBLEM SOLVING

Most of the academic people who heard Duke were more than sceptical, convinced that Duke was in over his head, but experts in the field of communications were much more responsive. A new government department, the Department of Communications, under Eric Kierans, staged a seminar at Carleton University in Ottawa, last May. The meeting was a "Seminar on access to information (the need to know) Telecommunications Study." Communications experts from industry, broadcasting and universities were invited to attend. Duke received an invitation to the sessions.

Duke asked two questions at the seminar that had the experts gasping. He asked if the information retrieval system for a proposed new data-bank would have information available to the Indian constituency and if that information would be relevant to the cultural perception of Indian people. The experts hadn't been thinking about that at all. Their whole system had been geared to the middle-class majority.

Duke's idea that any data system must include information relevant to cultural minorities in order to be an effective data system, simply hadn't been considered. The experts at the seminar considered the idea important enough to make it one of the six main topics discussed over the next three days.

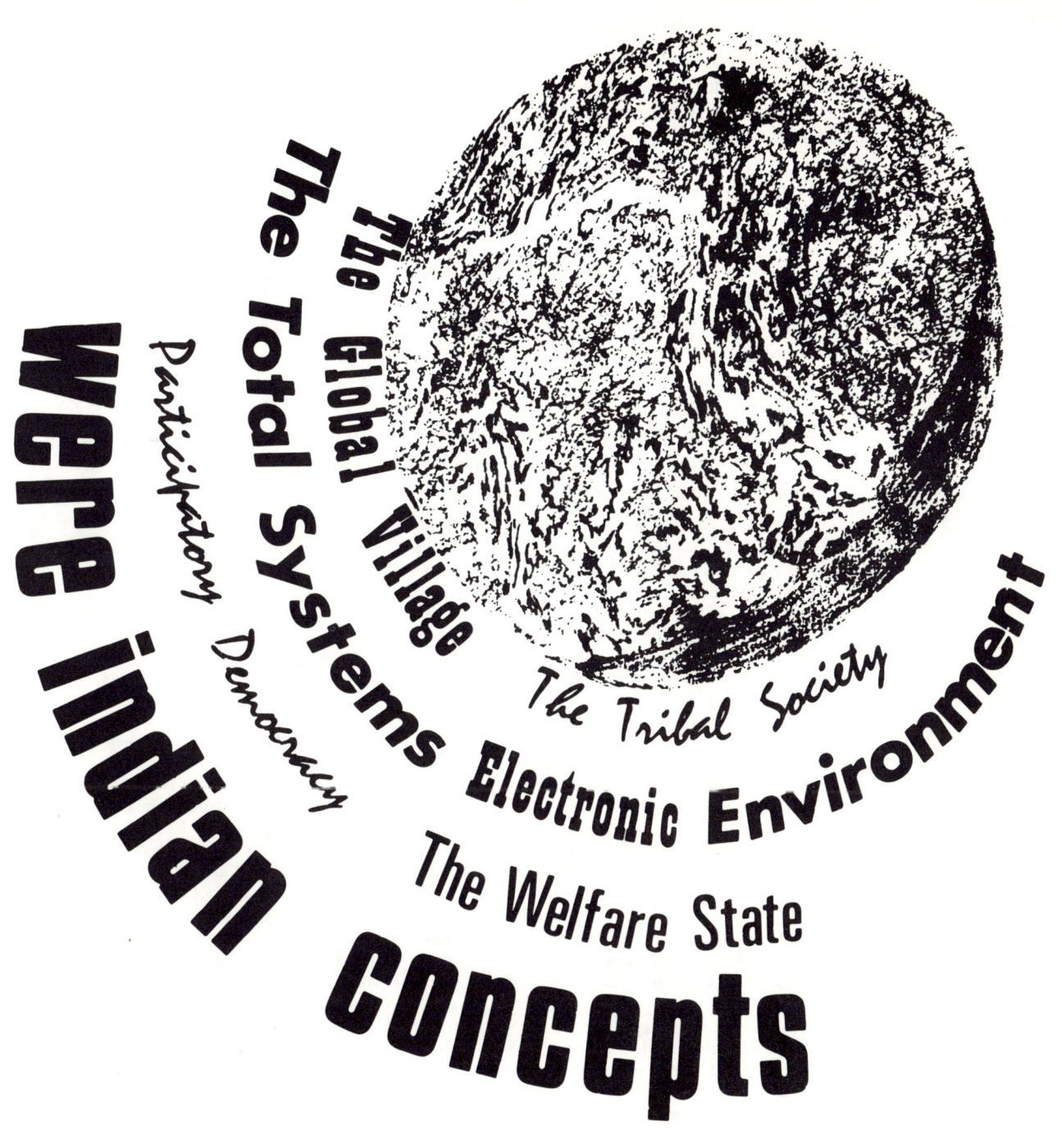

While Duke was working in *The Ecstasy of Rita Joe,* he fell in love with an actress in the cast, Sheila MacDonald. A teacher, an actress and a model, Sheila was, for Duke, the epitome of white womanhood. She was blond, green-eyed, and had all the finesse and social graces of an upper-middle-class debutante. Duke was smitten, in a word, and intimidated. Here, he thought, was his untouchable dream woman.

Duke hid his feelings during the run of *Rita Joe*, but on the final night, out of desperation, he simply reacted.

I was convinced if I didn't do something that night I would lose her. We left the theatre and I saw her getting into another car. I didn't know what to do. I ran up and grabbed her arm. "You're coming with me," I said, "I have to talk to you." I practically dragged her to the car. I started driving and just blurted out everything that came into my head. I told her I knew it was crazy, impossible and insane, but I loved her. When she told me she loved me too, I couldn't believe my ears. It really was too good to be true, but it was happening.

Sheila and I have lived together for almost a year now, and she has changed my life fantastically. Sure, the image thing was there at the beginning, but that isn't the potatoes of the relationship. I don't really know how to talk about love, because love is not a talking thing—it's a feeling thing. I'd lived with beautiful women before. They turned me on for a couple of weeks and that was it.

With Sheila there are so many levels of connection. She is the first girl I have ever been able to connect with on an intellectual level. We can talk in depth about anything we want to get into—and her ability to respond to my moods is incredible.

Elaine did this too, but she did it on an intuitive level. She provided a kind of solidity in my life and a sanctuary—a place I knew was there and could respond to; but she didn't have the same capacity for discussing what was happening.

Sheila and I have created a pattern or style of living. I can't even remember living in one place for a whole year, with the idea of living there for another year and another year, in the same place.

The biggest change is that Sheila is the first person I have ever been satisfied to be alone with. When we go out, or do things, the two of us are enough. I used to need a lot of people around me for stimulation, but Sheila provides it by herself.

There's an emotional level to me, and an intellectual level, that I keep separated. On an emotional level, there is a tremendous sense of warmth that comes over me when I am with Sheila. When we are involved together, when we do things together, when we walk down the street, or sit in the park, or have dinner, or sit at home watching television, there is a great emotional burden that is lifted from me.

There is a tremendous sense of warmth and security and love and all those things with an emotional base, but when there is a crisis and I have to make a choice, I don't make the choice on an emotional level—I discard the emotional portion because that happens to be the way I function. I just can't give total commitment. If I feel I'm being castrated creatively, I take off.

Sheila has been able to penetrate that space a little bit. As well as responding to her emotionally, I respond to her intellectually, and I've never had that with a woman before. When the emotional well has run dry there is still an intellectual level that I'm connected on. Elaine was completely out of her depth at that level.

The best description I've ever seen of the way I relate to women was in a book on Tecumtha where women are described as a flesh and blood code-book of the world we live in.

Some of the connections I make with women are made because there is a tremendous interest and excitement for me to connect with girls who embody a kind of space in life that I don't know very much about. In many ways my excitement with Elaine was on that kind of level, because she was a total code-book on the Indian space—much more so than Dorothy, for example.

Sheila complements me more than any other women I've known. She brings out the better side of me, and she is the first woman who has been able to make me think about myself. She can criticize what I do in a constructive way, and I've never been able to take criticism before.

What it amounts to, is that Sheila and I are very much alike in the way we think and the kinds of things we like to do. In her own world, she is quite successful in whatever she does. I respect her, you know? I see a lot of strength in her. I think she could handle crisis quite well and she has this ability to be patient and to continue working toward whatever goal she has pointed herself at.

I guess that sort of sums it up. I respect her as a woman, as a human being, and as a professional. The greatest thing about it is that she respects me and believes in my talents. Faith.

The kind of relationship that Sheila and I have, is the kind of relationship that will develop in the future, in North America. A male and a female can live together without being hung up on the social mores of it. Society will soon accept that people live like this.

I doubt that Sheila and I will reach the point where we can do it with complete freedom because we are victims of our backgrounds and experience, but our children will find it a more acceptable way of life.

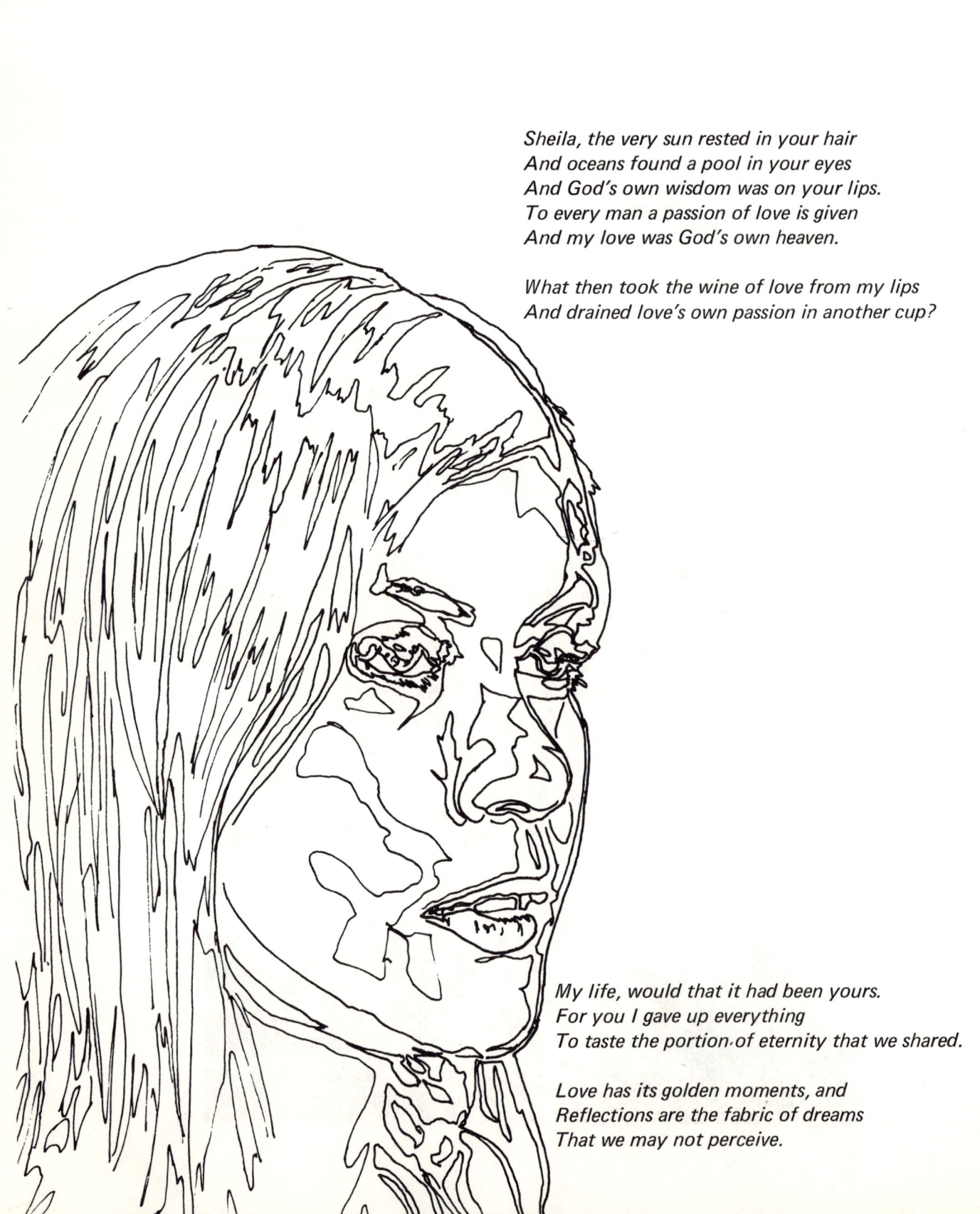

Sheila, the very sun rested in your hair
And oceans found a pool in your eyes
And God's own wisdom was on your lips.
To every man a passion of love is given
And my love was God's own heaven.

What then took the wine of love from my lips
And drained love's own passion in another cup?

My life, would that it had been yours.
For you I gave up everything
To taste the portion of eternity that we shared.

Love has its golden moments, and
Reflections are the fabric of dreams
That we may not perceive.

*Sheila is a river, softly flowing river.
I want to drown my sorrows
And the tears I have borrowed
From a thousand faces, that hide in empty places
In my mind.*

*Sheila had a moment, misty floating moment.
I want to embrace her with my eyes
And weave golden bracelets
Round her memories, frozen prematurely
In another prison, that lies locked securely
In the glaciers of my mind.*

*Sheila walks across an empty stage
That is filled with people.
She hands me silver raindrops in a crystal goblet.
I pour them in a lifespan between eternity and time
And feel my soul spinning in the delights
Of having touched my lips to a cup of
Forbidden wine.*

*Sheila sits beside me in the morning.
She holds an emerald teardrop in her hand.
And her words are like a fountain
Slowly folding back the midnight curtain
That cloaked our uncertain journey to this land.*

*High upon the mountain I see the clouds descending
And the shadows deep beneath them
Creep like extending fingers toward the silent valley
Of that fast-receding spirit that gave meaning
To my mind.*

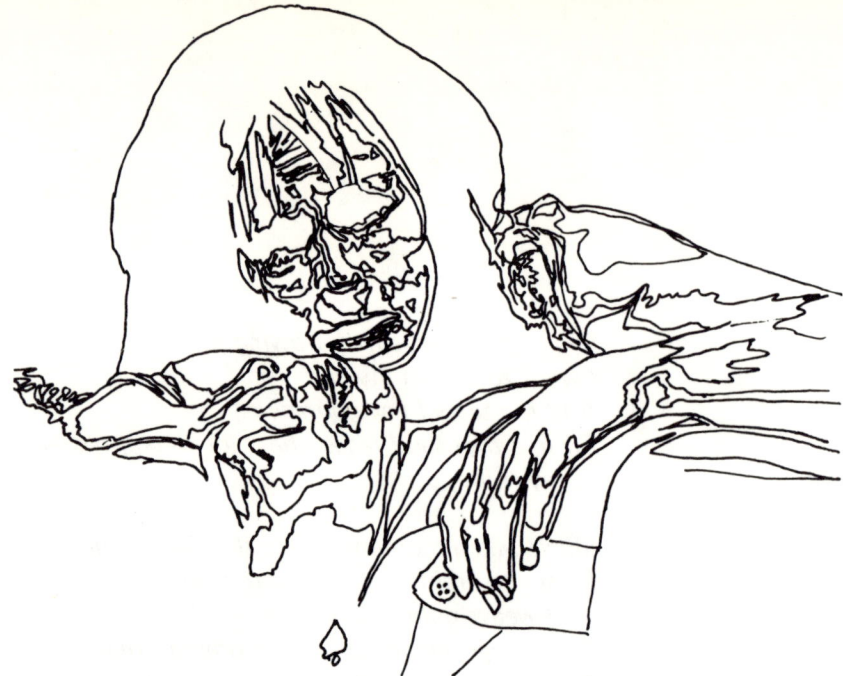

Especially intrigued by the idea of film as a medium, Duke began working out ideas for a film production. He decided on a full-length feature film on the life of Tecumtha, the Shawnee Indian leader who played a deciding role in the War of 1812. Duke took his idea to Ottawa and got the support of the Department of Indian Affairs. With that support, the National Film Board agreed to advance three thousand dollars for a treatment for the film.

Duke asked me to help with the research for the film, and as I began reading background material for the project, I was amazed by the uncanny parallels between the lives of Tecumtha and Duke.

Both had had their early lives altered by a disastrous fire; both had been educated to the white culture; both were poets, mystics, organizers, and orators, and both had a vision of the Indian's future in North America that called for a pan-Indian movement. My amazement doubled when I read translations of Tecumtha's speeches and discovered how similar their ideas were—sometimes right down to literal phrases—and Duke hadn't even seen the material yet.

The parallel lines met the day before these pages were written, when Duke discovered he is a great-great-great-great-grandson of Tecumtha.

A history department-head at Central Commerce, where Sheila was teaching dramatics, had spent his summer travelling among reserves gathering historical data on the Indians. He had visited the Saugeen reserve and interviewed Chief Jim Mason, Duke's uncle. Sheila, thinking Duke would be interested in the tape, brought it home. As Chief Mason related the history of his band and his family, he mentioned the hereditary link with Tecumtha. Duke had never known before that he was descended from Tecumtha..

Neither of us had ever written, or even seen a film treatment before but we knew what we wanted to get across and we sat down and went to work. A few weeks after we submitted the treatment Duke received his final installment of one thousand dollars. He called and was peculiarly insistent that I come down to the KNTV studios. Shortly after I arrived he casually pulled out a big roll of bills and counted off my share and handed it to me, saying:

Now we know what a film treatment is.

Shortly after we began the Tecumtha project, Duke received an invitation from the Winnipeg Indian Centre to take part in their Centennial Pageant and Indian Princess Pageant. We drove to Winnipeg, and for the first time I saw Duke's showbusiness trip in action.

One night, after the official festivities were over, we went to a party. Eventually I crawled into the back of the van and went to sleep. The next thing I heard was a growly voice saying, "OK you, out of the back of the truck." I opened my eyes, and was staring into the muzzle of a shotgun.

I scrambled out of the back of the truck and there were cops all over the place, all heavily armed, and all very unhappy. Duke was standing beside the truck, literally shaking. It had been a long night, his nerves were shot and he was afraid.

While Duke tried to explain who he was, detectives were ransacking the van. Duke showed the detectives a Canadian Magazine with a feature story about him and his Charlie Squash film. In the confusion, the police thought Duke was Charlie Squash and matters went from bad to worse. Duke looked so frightened, the police were convinced we must be hiding something.

Eventually the story came out that two policemen had been attacked, and one killed, a few hours before. Roadblocks were thrown up all over town and police were checking anything that moved.

Finally convinced that we weren't cop-killers, the police let us go. That night, the final night of the pageant, Duke was scheduled to do a stand-up comic routine as part of the show. He got on stage and right off the top of his head told the story of the "routine Winnipeg spot check" he had run into. The audience roared through the whole story. I was laughing so hard that I couldn't take any pictures. He had transformed that fear and confusion into an unroariously funny story. That took talent.

In show-business, people buy talent. They couldn't care less if you're a no-good bastard. If you can produce what the public likes, you're in business—if you can't, you're not. To have any staying power, you've got to have talent. One of the challenges was that by coming to Toronto and putting myself on the market, I was really pitting myself against the best that Canada had to offer. I found that I was competitive and that was a nice feeling, and still is.

The fact that show-business and revolution mixed so easily didn't surprise Duke, but it did cause a good deal of confusion. One weekend, Duke showed up in a new uniform. Despite the fact that he was wearing ordinary slacks and a shirt, a red beret sporting a target-design bead disk gave him a distinctly military look. Dark sunglasses and a black cigarette-holder completed the new Ché image.

To be a red-power militant in this country and the United States, is to be in showbusiness. If you get right down to it, Jerry Rubin and these other so-called revolutionaries, are nothing but show-business personalities. Their posturing in front of the camera is what their revolution really amounts to. If I were an honest

revolutionary or red-power militant, the last thing I would want is my picture in the paper.

If I'm fighting in a resistance movement and getting into that kind of bag, I don't particularly want everybody to know what I'm doing. If you are fighting in a resistance movement, you better be quiet about what you're doing.

I found it was dishonest of me to do red-power posturing and then not use some of my bread to buy guns and send them to places where they might be needed.

Duke's weekend Ché uniform had its effect. As he walked down the street, people stepped off the sidewalk to get out of his way. In the Celebrity Club, where Duke is a member, people just didn't know how to cope with him; then he just disappeared. He skipped to his houseboat near Sault Ste. Marie and no one heard from him for several weeks.

I WAS IN THE THROES OF NOT UNDERSTANDING WHAT I SHOULD DO AND WHAT I SHOULDN'T DO. I HAD A LOT OF PRESSURE ON ME, FROM PEOPLE AROUND ME, TO DO SOMETHING—AND I HAD NO IDEA WHAT IT WAS, AND I WAS STILL TRYING TO FIGURE IT OUT.

When I'm really sailing and going on in an ideal sort of way, I start feeling myself being pulled down, and when I'm on a down trip, I can feel the forces that are bringing me up. It goes like that, in cycles.

As hard as this may be to believe, there is very little that I do with an ulterior motive. It has got me into a lot of trouble. One week, I may really believe in the direction I'm moving and that, at the time, the things I am doing and saying are really the truth; but in the light of new experience, all that can change.

I roll intuitively with events. I don't really shape events. Events very often determine what I do, although the very action of what I do creates the other events, that later cause me to change direction and do something different.

I had no idea of the amount of influence I really have on people. In the last ten years, I really wasn't consciously aware of how seriously people took what I said and did. For instance, I go to this conference and because of the unreality of the whole situation, I begin to think of the conference as a stage. And I'm just going to be an actor for three days, and make statements, do spacy kinds of things—not realizing that everybody is taking all this very seriously.

Very often, I don't take myself very seriously. A good deal of what I do, I do for fun. If it wasn't fun, I wouldn't do it. When something gets to be routine and drudgery, I get turned off. And then all kinds of people—

For instance, at the Thunderbird: I get that going and all kinds of things are happening and everybody is excited, but then people start connecting to it as a permanent fixture in their lives. And then I drop out and everybody gets uptight.

They say, "Christ, here I've committed myself to something and worked for it, and he's just using it as a stepping-stone to his next project."

They have what they call a real commitment, where I was just creating a play and we were all players, and actors, and I walk away from it and people get angry. I never realized how serious my spaces were to other people.

If ever my way was the way that caused pain;
If ever my words felt empty and were hollow;
If ever my hands touched soft flesh and were cold;
If ever my heart spoke lies and stopped beating;
Forgive me.

Not because of my human and selfish weakness;
Not because of my pride that seeks humouring;
Not because of my stature that would not stoop;
Not because of my heart that broke a long time past:

Forgive me
For the sunshine that warmed our souls;
For the fragrance of the flowers that we picked;
For the radiance of moonlight on still bodies;
For the splash of a thousand rivers that we crossed;
Forgive me.

IT'S REALLY DIFFICULT TO PIN DOWN WHAT I'M DOING AT SOME PERIODS BECAUSE IT'S DIFFICULT TO SEPARATE THE FANTASY FROM THE REALITY.

I didn't realize that this is what people call conning. Because looking back over my life, I tried to figure out how people really got conned, how they really got screwed. None of them got screwed for money, it was always in terms of emotion, in terms of commitment.

Tobacco burns when touched by fire
The smoke rises up up, Blue & Grey
A fog that holds medicine
The spirit is strong, the story is old
The smoke curls.
I feel a sound, the sound of drums
on distant hills, buffalo hoofs on
      frozen ground
A medicine chant wailing by
   breezes that have not blown
     for many moons nor
      suns that shine
      no longer on
      brown children
      my eyes seek
      a vision for
      old people
      told of visions
      that were not
      seen by eyes
      but burned in
     the mind and mouth
      of our men who
     fought battles but
      did not win.
My body cries for strong medicine
But my eyes water from whiskey
My brain bleeds, my heart sweats
I regret, that tobacco burns and
I am not strong.

JOHN REDBIRD
1970

Following a three-week retreat on his houseboat, Duke returned to Toronto with the first act of a two-act play that explores the relationship of the Indian to himself and to the modern world, particularly to the computer. Duke put out feelers for people interested in forming a company to stage the play. Response was immediate.

Ron Singer, Director of the Stratford Workshop Productions, David Haber of the National Arts Centre in Ottawa and choreographer Garbut Roberts were all interested in getting the production on the road. George Yost of Project Planners forecast a budget of fifty thousand dollars for the show, and Duke is presently raising money for its production.

During the retreat, Duke had been thinking, too, of his experiences in show business. He feared that even here, he would be boxed and confined to a mould or a role.

The myth in showbusiness is that the people who are on camera have the power and that the people who do the production are just tools to allow the people in front to do their trip. I took a look at what happened to some of the people who thought this way. It occurred to me that I was on the wrong side of the camera.

Remember Laurier LaPierre, Stanley Burke and Patrick Watson? These three men really believed they had power because they were on camera. They tried to exercise that power. LaPierre and Watson got into politics and Burke got into the Biafra thing. As soon as they began to go against the establishment, they were dropped off-camera. They were unable to function.

The three of them without the camera are nothing, nonentities like the rest of us: so the executive producer, who controls the camera, makes or breaks the star.

The big mistake was that these guys believed that they had a following, and they could use this following to get into politics. It just doesn't work that way.

I saw that the producer of a show could make Jerry Rubin look like a big clown or a highly sensitive individual; if I fell out of favour with the media, they could do to me what they did to Kantineta Horn. Ronald Reagan had to get right out of movies and establish a different kind of power-base to be Governor of California.

Unless your whole trip just happens to be that you want to be on camera and be in the grip of the media all the time, then you have to get into your own production and do your own thing. I really want to do my own productions because I have something to say.

Duke had reached a focus, or nexus, in his experience. The duality of white and red were fusing into a synthesis. All that remained was to find the medium to express it.

What I have to say is that the world we live in today, the electronic, tribal, total-systems, cybernetic society, is the real manifestation of the Indian personality. We no longer have to live in the woods and isolate ourselves from North American society. What we have to do is go out into the world and become the manifestation of what the real North American is going to become—the ideal, whole man. We, as Indians, can represent the best possible example of what everyone in America will eventually become.

Silent flies the hawk by night,
Silent float the clouds in flight,
Silent stands the mountain tall,
Silent is my sparrow's fall.

Halfway across an ocean wide
Halfway up the jagged mountain side
Halfway to a fountain in Rome,
Halfway to my sparrow's home.

Laughter in the darkness deep
Laughter in a dream-filled sleep
Laughter all intensified
Laughter is my sparrow's cry.

THE WESTERN EUROPEAN MAN HAS IMPREGNATED THE WOMB OF NORTH AMERICA WITH THE SPERM OF TECHNOLOGY. THAT TECHNOLOGY HAS FERTILIZED THE EGG WITHIN THE WOMB AND WILL PRODUCE A NEW NORTH AMERICAN MAN, WITH THE BEST FEATURES OF BOTH WORLDS IN HIS PERSONALITY. THE ORIGINAL ACT, THE ORIGINAL RELATIONSHIP, WAS A RAPE. THE NEW RELATIONSHIP MUST BE A FAMILY—A TRIBE.

> My role in this tribe is as a messenger, a catalyst. I'm just beginning that trip now. Before that, I was opening doors. My accomplishment to date has been to make it through the labyrinth of the physical, mental and spiritual fire that one has to walk through, in order to become hardened or purified enough to do the other job.
>
> It's not a fate or destiny trip. I may be preordained to do those things, but it is my choice to do them. I can cop out tomorrow, but somebody else will take my place and do the job. Many are called, but few are chosen: and that really gives you a sense of responsibility. But it's my choice, really.

Duke's opportunity was quick to show itself. Convinced that he had to be able to produce his own programs to say what he wanted to say, he explored the possibilities of video-tape recording, and the possibilities seemed endless.

Duke had several meetings with Noel Moore, then vice-president of programming for Cablecasting Limited, in Ottawa. Mr. Moore offered Duke an entire channel to be devoted to Indian Broadcasting. That was all Duke needed.

Within three weeks, he had pulled enough equipment together to set up a complete VTR mobile unit. Kukewium Native Broadcasting was becoming a reality. The rest of the Redbird story will have to be told on your television screen.

> **AT ONE TIME, I REALLY BELIEVED THAT TO BE AN INDIAN I HAD TO HAVE ALL THE INDIAN ATTACHMENTS. I BELIEVED THAT IN ORDER TO BE ACCEPTED AS AN INDIAN I WOULD HAVE TO HAVE AN INDIAN WIFE AND INDIAN CHILDREN, AND LIVE WITH INDIANS, AND REJECT ALL WHITE VALUES. BUT NOW, I CAN BE COMPLETELY FREE.**
>
> **I DEFY ANYBODY TO SAY THAT I'M LESS OF AN INDIAN BECAUSE I'M LIVING IN A WHITE WORLD. COMMENTS LIKE, "YOU'RE A WHITE MAN NOW," WOULD HAVE BEEN DEVASTATING FOR ME FIVE YEARS AGO. TODAY I'D LAUGH AT THEM. I KNOW WHO I AM, AND WHATEVER I DO, I'M DOING AS AN INDIAN. I NO LONGER INTEND TO LIVE AS OTHER PEOPLE WANT ME TO LIVE—ANY OTHER PEOPLE. I'LL LIVE AS I WANT TO LIVE.**

Nishnaba Nishnaba Nishnaba NISHNABA Nishnaba
Nishnaba I am Nishnaba
I am Ojibway which means We are the People
Nishnaba NISHNABA
Nishnaba
Nishnaba
Nishnaba

NISHNABA

*I shall make of thee a rare wine
That is not squeezed from grapes
Neither is it crushed from fruit
Nor brewed from any herb
Nor held in any vessel,
Except it be the vessel of life itself.*

*I shall make of thee a rare wine
And this wine shall be in no way cast out,
For your body shall be its vessel,
And your life its flavour.
And if they shall taste of your body
But perceive not the wine
Then it shall be like unto bitter lemon
And their mouths shall reject thy person
And their tongues shall spit thy liquid
As a deadly poison.
For their tongues shall be accursed before the Lord
For I have made of you a peculiar person
And your wine shall be for them that are in darkness.
Then shall you be like a thorn that shall tear the flesh,
And I will bring confusion unto their spirits.
And they shall raise up their voices against you
And they shall heap vileness and abuse of every manner upon you.
Despair not, for I have yet to bring you to the fullness
Of your days, and neither have you entered into the dispensation
For which you were born and have come among men.*

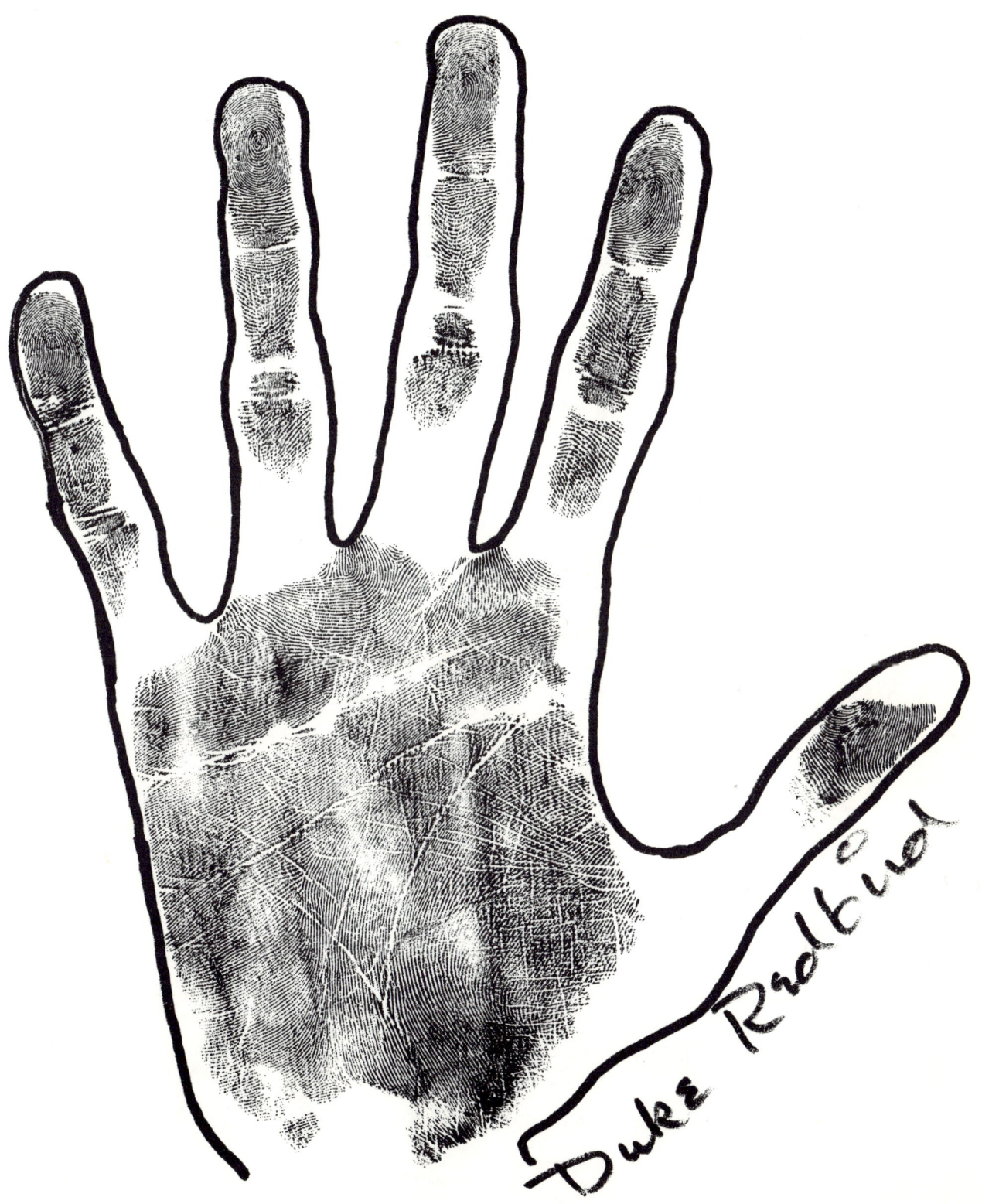